T0280109

THE
GEORGIA
FARMERS' STRIKE

THE AMERICAN AGRICULTURAL MOVEMENT VS. JIMMY CARTER

LEE LANCASTER

THE
History
PRESS

Published by The History Press
Charleston, SC
www.historypress.com

Copyright © 2023 by Lee Lancaster
All rights reserved

First published 2023

Manufactured in the United States

ISBN 9781467154253

Library of Congress Control Number: 2023932153

Notice: The information in this book is true and complete to the best of our knowledge. It is offered without guarantee on the part of the author or The History Press. The author and The History Press disclaim all liability in connection with the use of this book.

All rights reserved. No part of this book may be reproduced or transmitted in any form whatsoever without prior written permission from the publisher except in the case of brief quotations embodied in critical articles and reviews.

To my wife and children, Keri, Nate and Caroline.

Praise God from whom all blessings flow.

CONTENTS

Contents

ACKNOWLEDGEMENTS

P eople ask me where to find information about the farmers' strike. I tell them to find a farmer who was born before 1954. Most of the information in this book was obtained from interviews I conducted over the phone or at the kitchen table. First, I asked my daddy about it. Then I asked Sonny Stapleton. And then I asked Agriculture Commissioner Gary Black; he told me about a fellow named Terrell Hudson. Terrell and Mrs. Alice Hudson really opened up the door to what was the farmers' strike. They knew a fellow named Tommy Kersey and all the county coordinators for the American Agriculture Movement. Then I read a book called *From the White House to the Hoosegow*. Mentioned in this book is a man from Alma named Tommy Carter. I called Chris Carter, who got me in touch with Tommy Carter's son, Thomas Carter. It went from there.

Thanks to all the people who shared their lives, stories and pictures with me.

The farmers: Ronnie Lancaster (my daddy), Sonny Stapleton, Terrell Hudson, Marvin Trice, Gerald Richardson, Winston Miles, Albert and Ann Wildes, Bobby Browning, Bruce Veal, Carden Summers, Chris Carter, William Scott, Danny Anderson, David Miller, David Senter, Pat West, David West, Earl Barlow, Eddie Lewis, Ellis Black, Ernie Selph, Carey Knowles, Garland White, Milton Ussery, Gerald Long, Johnny Colston, Monty Spinks, Rex Bullock, Tom Herrington and Mimi, Wendell Kersey and John Nutt.

Their families: Thomas Carter, Leonard Hill, Ben Boyd, Benji Anderson, Russ Goodman, Michael Morgan, Nancyanne Conner, Richard Andel,

Steve Short, Terry Sims, Thor Brannen, Trent Williams, Jim Tripp and Betty Jean Milford.

The agribusiness and law enforcement folks: Don Giles, T.E. Moye, Sheriff Ed Coley, Agriculture Commissioner Gary Black, Peyton Sapp (UGA Extension, Burke County), Sheriff Kris Coody and Paul Thompson.

From Georgia State Patrol: Colonel Chris Wright, Sergeant First Class Hamilton Halford, Russ Abernathy (GSP, retired), Trooper First Class Timmy Lowe.

The papers: the *Statesboro Herald*; the *Telfair Enterprise*; the Ocmulgee Regional Library; the Tift County Library (*Tifton Gazette* archive); the Pulaski County Clerk's Office (the *Hawkinsville Dispatch* archive); the staff at the *Cochran Journal*, Brandy, Tammy and Taylor; Amy Carter and the *Market Bulletin*; Erin White and *Georgia Grown*; and Ellie Loudermilk and the Perry Area Historical Museum.

Thanks to Ms. Starks for teaching me how to read, Mrs. Long for teaching me how to write, Dr. Elder for teaching me how to write something people could read and Mama for making me go to school.

INTRODUCTION

Throe most expensive trip to Atlanta I ever took." That's how the tractorcade in 1977 was described in a Facebook post I saw a couple of years ago. It got the discussion going between me and my daddy, who had attended the rally at the capital before I was born. He dropped pieces of the story whenever it came to mind, like when it was unseasonably cold or during the trucker strike in Ottawa that drew numerous comparations to the big D.C. tractorcade in '79. I finally got the whole story from him and a lot of other farmers over the course of a couple of months, and I found almost everyone who was old enough—and some who weren't—to have made their way to Capitol Hill that day. Not everyone's story was the same—nor was their path to the Georgia Capitol or their opinion of the rally. But everyone was there for one reason: farming was about to fall off a cliff if nothing was done.

I started researching this story after the trucker strike in Ottawa. I had never seen anything about a farmer strike when I was at Abraham Baldwin Agricultural College (ABAC) in Tifton or the University of Georgia (UGA) in Athens. In all the years I had worked for the Georgia Department of Agriculture, I had never heard a word about it.

I loved researching this book. I loved talking to the farmers involved. I now love talking to folks about what I've learned. Some of the strikers left this subject in the past because it didn't turn out like it should have. We lost a lot of jobs and a lot of farms. A lot of farmers lost their way of life. But they stood up and fought for what they thought was right. And that is a story that needs to be told from the Oil Lamp Restaurant to the Funston Café—over and over again.

1

GIMME JIMMY!

Farmers aren't protesters. They aren't picketers, either. But they do speak their minds when the need arises. When the country was formed, it was formed by farmers with homes built on farms called Mount Vernon and Monticello. If they didn't farm before the war with the British, they farmed afterward. The farmers' influence in Washington diminished with their numbers over time, and in the 1970s, they had completely lost their foothold in Washington, Atlanta and everywhere else it seemed. Young men lamented that they used to brag about being farmers, but by the late '70s, they hoped no one would ask what they did for a living in a social setting.

When the '70s began, commodity prices were strong. Land prices were fair, and newfangled farm equipment that made life easier was being introduced almost daily. Horses and mules were replaced with tractors after World War II. Self-propelled combines replaced the primitive threshers that had been invented one hundred years before and were powered by steam. Tillage implements, like harrows and plows, grew from repurposed, mule-drawn antiques into four-row, six-row and eight-row models. The wider the plows got, the larger the tractors grew. In the Great Plains, tractors the size of schoolhouses pulled plows that could tear up some fields in Georgia in one pass. Eventually, Georgia fields grew and so did the tractors.

With higher horsepower came higher payments. The John Deere B, credited with being the model that replaced draft animals on the farm, cost less than $800 in 1939. By 1949, the price of the tractor had doubled to over $1,600, due mostly to the price of steel after America left millions of tons of it strewn across battlefields in faraway places like El Alamein and Bastogne and on the bottom of the ocean at Midway and Leyte Gulf. The next, larger model that came along was part of the New Generation, the John Deere 4020 of the 1960s. It was sold for around $12,000. When the Next Generation 4430 with the Sound-Gard body came out, it rang up at over twice the price, at around $27,000. The 4430 had a lot more power and some things no one had seen before: a cab, air-conditioning and a radio. While interest rates were over 15 percent, most agricultural equipment could be purchased with interest rates around 4 percent. It was still hard to make a profit, since the fields, yields, fuel consumption and commodity prices didn't change just because the overhead costs went up.

A good example of how cost of living had gone up was told to me by Pat West from Pinehurst: "John Deere had come out with the 30 Series tractors and was demonstrating them all over the state. I went to Statesboro and saw them work at the dealership over there. I came home and told my wife I had to have them. She said, 'If you'll build me a house, you can get the tractors.' So, I did. And I moved up from four-row equipment to six-row. I traded a 4020 for a 4430 and a 8430. The interest wasn't but about 4 percent, but it was still hard to cover."

Other farmers were finding it a little too easy to get in over their heads. One farmer told me the John Deere dealer wouldn't accept a FmHA check at the time, but the International Harvester dealer met him at the door. "I bought a brand-new 1486 with three or four implements for what the Deere would have cost me. And they took my FmHA check."

During the Nixon and Ford administrations, the U.S. secretary of agriculture was Earl Butz. The collapse in commodity prices has been attributed to his advice to farmers to plant just about every inch of their farms. His undersecretary was former Georgia agriculture commissioner Phil Campbell. Butz was a capitalist with one goal in mind: get the government out of the farming business. He succeeded in removing price supports for everything but peanuts and rice while telling farmers to plant more or do something else. The effect of planting fencerow to fencerow without price supports was an overstock of commodities and pre–World War I prices that would last for nearly a decade.

Even the weatherman was against the farmer in 1977. One of the worst droughts set in on Georgia that year and didn't let go until the corn had been pulled. Almost all the cropland in Georgia at the time was dryland or unirrigated. What the drought didn't get, southern corn blight destroyed. Ellis Black, a former senator from Lowndes County, recalled:

> We had the southern corn blight hit our corn. The whole country's agriculture took a dadgum hit, but we took the double hit because, with that corn blight, we didn't make much corn, but then what we did make ended up getting aflatoxin in it. I think the motivating factor behind the federal government coming around with a disaster program was the aflatoxin in the corn. Corn was much bigger in South Georgia's agriculture at that time than it is today. Soybeans hadn't gotten their foot in the door good. There were a few soybeans being grown, but it wasn't until after '77 when we started planting soybeans. There were still just a few counties growing cotton. So South Georgia, for the most part, grew peanuts, tobacco and corn—and pastured hogs and cows—and a few pecans.

That year, Georgia produced eighty million bushels of corn less than the year before, one-fifth of the previous year's crop. The total farm income of the state fell 40 percent from the previous year, even with an increase in production acreage.

The commodity prices were an insult. The price paid at the buying point took care of roughly 60 percent of the cost of production. Though Georgia had a bad year, the Midwest brought in a bumper crop. According to the USDA, the average price for a bushel of wheat was $2.33, corn was $2.05 and soybeans were $5.88. Currently, wheat is averaging $8.00, corn is $6.00 and soybeans are $13.50. From the 1970s to now, wheat yields have gone from 30 bushels per acre to about 48; corn has nearly doubled from 90 to about 175; and soybeans have gone from around 30 to over 50. As an example of what the farmers were facing, a 100-acre crop of wheat cost $11,650 to produce in the spring of 1977. A farmer could expect a payment of $6,990 after the crop was sold, taking a loss of $4,660. For 100 acres of corn, an investment of $30,750 would yield $18,450, a loss of $12,300. For 100 acres of soybeans, an investment of $40,500 would bring in $29,400, a loss of $11,100.

In November 1976, the country had elected Jimmy Carter as president. All of Georgia and farming country had great expectations of Jimmy, a peanut farmer from Plains, Georgia. He and his young brother, Billy, came up the hard way during the boll weevil era in the lean years prior to World War II. His family grew cotton, tobacco and peanuts, and Jimmy and Billy provided the labor. Jimmy had also served as FFA president while attending

Plains High School. After graduation, he joined the navy and served on a nuclear-powered submarine until the call came from Plains that his father had died unexpectedly. Jimmy and his wife, Rosalyn, moved back home to help run the family business, a peanut buying point in town.

Carter began serving on the county school board and ran for the Georgia State Senate in the early 1960s. In 1970, he ran for governor and beat the Republican challenger, Hal Suit, by a country mile. During Carter's single term as governor in 1973, the Watergate scandal broke and was litigated on national television in the U.S. Senate by a lawyer from Lovejoy named Herman Talmadge. The president at

Jimmy Carter, the thirty-ninth president of the United States. *Author's collection.*

the time, Richard Nixon, stepped down and handed the keys of *Air Force One* to Gerald Ford. No one knew who he was because, even though Nixon had won forty-nine out of fifty states in 1972, Ford's name wasn't on the ballot. Spiro Agnew, who ran for vice president on the Nixon ticket in 1972, had to resign after being convicted of tax evasion. American politics were becoming a mess.

The Democrats knew that victory in 1976 was a lock, but the primaries for their nominee lingered on through the summer in a two-horse race between the former governor of Georgia and his complete opposite, the former governor of Alabama, George Wallace. Using imagery of smiling peanuts and a campy Georgian with a big ol' toothy smile, Carter ran his campaign out of the railroad depot beside the SAM rail line in downtown Plains with the help of an ever-present stray dog and a rotary dial telephone. After finally conquering Wallace in late summer, the Carter campaign rolled full steam ahead to meet Gerald Ford head on. When the votes were in, Jimmy Carter defeated the fatally unpopular Ford by a landslide, and Georgia sent its first president to the White House. Hope was in the air across farming country.

Sonny Stapleton from nearby Weston, Georgia, had a unique perspective of the situation that only a southwest Georgia farmer could have:

I knew Billy better than I knew Jimmy, but I knew Jimmy because he got to be governor. Then he left the country boys. I reckon he did, 'cause I didn't see him anymore. But we went to the inauguration, and I was singing that song, "Gimme Jimmy! Gimme Jimmy!" but Jimmy didn't do much for us. We certainly had hope, but hope never did come around! We had hope.

They had a reception the day before the inauguration, and we went. When we went to the inauguration, we got to the hotel, and something was wrong with the heat. We had to stay in Alexandria. They asked us not to have cameras and all that, but this friend of mine was along there, and he was in the line just before Paula and I. We had gone into business as a competitor to Jimmy. He had gone into the peanut business in Plains, and we had gone into buying peanuts in Weston.

My friend Harold told Jimmy, 'Watch that fella behind you. He's your competitor." He turned around and made our picture. I don't know where that picture is. It used to be hanging on my wall of us shaking hands with the president of the United States. And that's the only president I ever shook hands with.

Secretary of Agriculture Robert Bergland was a United States representative from Roseau, Minnesota. He had won his seat as a Democrat earlier in the decade, after rising through the ranks of the USDA's Agricultural Stabilization and Conservation Service in his home state. Many people have asked how he came to be appointed the secretary of agriculture, since the president was a farmer from Plains, Georgia. Secretary Bergland had served in the Minnesota delegation with a senator who had just been elected vice president named Walter Mondale.

As soon as the 1976 presidential election was over, the U.S. Congress began formulating the 1977 Farm Bill. During the drafting of the bill, the government, including the newly elected president, appeared to be tone

Jimmy Carter's presidential campaign headquarters, the depot in downtown Plains, in 1976. *Author's collection.*

deaf to what the farm bill was going to spell out for farmers. The loan level, which established the rock-bottom price of each commodity, was set to guarantee a loss for the next four years. The remedy from the government was loans. No one wanted more loans, because they had to be paid back at some point. If the commodity prices weren't going to cover the cost of production for the next four years, there wouldn't be any money left at the end of the season to pay back the loans.

Robert Bergland, USDA secretary from 1977 to 1981 during the Carter administration. *USDA.*

On March 19, 1977, Secretary Bergland publicly announced a proposal to cut peanut price supports by 20 percent and allotment acreage by 30 percent over four years. The president told Bergland to formulate the reductions without his input. With hundreds of peanut farmers living in the same zip code as the president, this news came as the first sign of trouble ahead. Why did the president ask to stay out of the negotiations? Either he knew the cuts had to be made and didn't want to let his emotions get in the way, or he wanted a scapegoat in Secretary Bergland. Either way, the law stated commodity prices for peanuts must remain above 75 percent of parity.

Also tucked into the farm bill was a word most folks had never heard of: *parity*. Albert Einstein once said, "If you can't explain something plainly, you don't know enough about it." *Parity* has always been a difficult word to plainly explain. Parity is a formula found in the Aiken Farm Act of 1948 that calculates the break-even price for a given commodity, plus a profit amount. To calculate parity, one must take the ten-year average price of a commodity and divide it by the average price of fifty-six domestic commodities over the same ten-year period. Then they must multiply that number by the current price index paid by farmers for inputs, adjusted against the same inputs' prices from 1910 to 1914. Each crop's ten-year average and inputs were different, so the parity price was different. The formula provided parity, or a fair price, for a commodity on par with the value of money collected around 1914. The farm bill said commodity prices would be set at 90 percent parity if there was a shortage of that crop. Parity, even at 90 percent, was way more than the price they were getting. For the same wheat crop bringing $2.33 a bushel, it would bring over $5.50

a bushel at 100 percent parity. Corn, at $2.05, would be worth over $3.50 with full parity. The simplest way parity was explained in terms of value was done by Gerald Long, former Georgia Farm Bureau president: "It's the difference between a 1964 quarter and a 1965 quarter. A 1964 quarter is worth a lot because it's made out of silver. A 1965 quarter is worth a quarter because it's made outta…nothing."

2

A FARMERS' STRIKE IS ORDERED
AT THE CHUCK WAGON CAFÉ

T he 1977 Farm Bill was becoming a reality and was certain to be signed by the president after it passed the U.S. House and Senate. If it went into effect in January 1978, farmers would have to live with it until 1982, so they had to do something fast. The House of Representatives and Senate were controlled by Democrats with a two-thirds majority in both houses after the tidal wave of Democratic support in down ballot races in 1976 after the Watergate scandal took down President Richard Nixon. The entire Georgia delegation of ten congressmen and two senators were Democrats. The speaker of the house was Tip O'Neill of Massachusetts, and future House Speaker Tom Foley of Washington was serving as the Agriculture Committee chairman. Dawson Mathis from Nashville, Georgia, served as the ranking member from South Georgia's Second District. The Senate majority leader was Robert Byrd of West Virginia, with Herman Talmadge of Georgia serving as the Senate Agriculture Committee chairman.

During the summer of 1977, a small group of farmers started discussing a strike at a café, presumably the Chuck Wagon Café, at a crossroads in Springfield, Colorado. The group of farmers, the founding fathers of what would become the American Agriculture Movement, included the café's owner, Alvin Jenkins, Jerry Wright, Greg Suhler and brothers Bud and Lynn Bittner and Gene, Darrel and Billy Schroder. The area was rural, where the foothills of the Rocky Mountains transitioned into the wheat field of the Great Plains. In the middle of these amber waves of grain sat the café at a busy intersection of two federal highways leading to Amarillo, Dodge City,

American Agriculture Movement patch. *Author's collection.*

Santa Fe and Denver, and it was frequented by union truckers familiar with the tactics used to picket employers, as they had been involved in several strikes conducted earlier in the decade. The farmers knew that something drastic had to be done to get the public's and government's attention, and the truckers knew how to get it.

The farmers in Springfield contacted their congressman in Washington, Jim Johnson, to set up a meeting with Secretary Bergland. They were told that Bergland had a campaign stop to stump for another Colorado congressman scheduled that very week in Denver. The farmers requested time to voice their opposition to the new farm bill but were told that the secretary's trip had been scheduled from top to bottom with no extra time to meet with them. After some persuading, Bergland recanted with an offer to meet them in Denver. Since he was the secretary of agriculture, he probably needed to meet with some farmers now and again. The farmers asked him to travel to Springfield to hear from them on their turf. After more negotiations, Bergland and the farmers settled on a meeting in Pueblo, Colorado, around halfway between Springfield and Denver.

Over the next few days, the small group of farmers burned up the phone lines and recruited farmers throughout the region. They pushed, pulled and parked their tractors along the major highways leading to Denver and Pueblo, with signs displaying the plight that was occurring and threats of a farmers' strike. This small group grew to include several thousand farmers in just a few days, with farmers reaching out on landline telephones (fifteen years before Al Gore invented the internet). The farmers used a phone tree to get the word out quickly. One farmer would call six people in an hour, while everybody he called would call six people. Talking about how quickly the farmers could get the word out, David Senter said, "We'd have really been dangerous if we had social media and cellphones back then!"

September 22, 1977, the scheduled meeting date, arrived with the very first tractorcade of the farmers' movement forming the day before. Like a web throughout the Great Plains, thousands of farmers with tractors and pickup trucks lined up from Amarillo to Kansas—even some from the secretary's home state of Minnesota inched toward Pueblo. Robert Bergland held up his end of the bargain, arriving at a different meeting place than originally planned due to the overwhelming crowd. For several hours inside

Pueblo Memorial Hall, the secretary sat through one impassioned speech after another from the broke farmers of the Great Plains and their wives. When the dust settled, Bergland rose from his seat and told the crowd he could not work miracles, and he left the auditorium without giving any promises or any hope. His position on the farm bill was firm. As written, the bill was as good as it was going to get. He and President Carter believed any increase in price support would cause the economy to fall into a depression. The reason for such fear was that the economy was wilting under inflation rates that were soaring around 20 percent.

Secretary Bergland boarded his plane back to D.C. while the farmers mounted their tractors to head downhill toward home, completely deflated. At eighteen miles per hour and nearly two hundred miles from home, the farmers had plenty of time to think and plan. When they got home, they put a plan in place to strike. But the strike wouldn't be effective if only the farmers from Denver to Lubbock participated. Teams of speakers went out and crisscrossed farm country to gain support and tell the story of the farm bill and the Pueblo rally. With each rally came new recruits who went back to speak to farmers in uncharted places, where folks chewed tobacco and knew the difference between Cal Smith and Carl Smith.

Something called the American Agriculture Movement and a farmers' strike were talked about at every dime store, feed store, feed lot and parking lot from San Antonio, Texas, to Saginaw, Michigan. *Parity* was the new buzzword, scribbled on grain bins and handmade signs that were taped to tractors strategically placed on the roadside, and then the term made it onto buttons and bumper stickers. The AAM began to establish itself in rural communities, with new strike offices popping up and rallies being held farther and farther from the little corner stop in Colorado. The goal of the AAM was to gain leverage in commodity pricing to at least break even by threatening a strike starting on December 14. Farmers planned to not buy materials, such as fuel, seed and fertilizer; not sell any crops or livestock; and not plant anything if they didn't get legislation to see prices increase.

Throughout September and early October 1977, rallies, parades and tractorcades were organized throughout the Midwest. Some of the farmers noticed there wasn't much noise being made in Georgia. So, two farmers from Plains, Kansas, Gene Short and Bill Fox, reached out to a farmer named James Short in Plains, Georgia, and told him how powerful his town's influence could be if there was a protest against his neighbor Jimmy Carter. James Short put the Kansas farmers in touch with a young man from Unadilla named Tommy Kersey.

Many of the folks around Plains were still fond of the president, as they still are today. Many of the area's farmers did business with the Carters and attended church with them. Billy Carter ran a gas station that still stands as it did in its glory days in Plains. No Georgia fireplace mantel is complete without a forty-something-year-old 1980 Georgia National Championship Coke bottle and at least one can of Billy Beer. Billy and Jimmy's mother, Lillian, was still up and about at the time, along with their sister Gloria. Their cousin Hugh Carter was the district's state senator, and he had made a name for himself as one of the largest bait cricket and worm producers in the country.

The first official American Agriculture Movement meeting was recalled to me by one of the attendees, Rex Bullock: "The first meeting we had when we started with Tommy Kersey and the AAM was at Mr. Sam Thompson's shelter on the Wilcox/Pulaski County line. That's where the first meeting was held in Georgia."

In the middle of the largest cotton producing region in the state and along the paths of two major highways, I-75 and U.S. 41, sits Dooly County. Unadilla, Pinehurst and Vienna became the centers of the farm strike universe and were just as active as the groups in Colorado and Amarillo. The motor that gave life to the show was Tommy Kersey from Henderson. He and his two brothers, Leighton and Wendell, farmed about five thousand acres on the Houston County line with their father, Charlie. Tommy and Leighton were in every picture and quoted in every farmers' strike story from late 1977 throughout the life of the American Agriculture Movement in Georgia. Tommy Kersey had just recently served as Dooly County president of the Jaycees organization and obtained his leadership skills through the Jaycees' "Speak Up" program. If a movie was made about Tommy Kersey's life, he would be portrayed by Paul Newman but with Jimmy Swaggart as his stunt double. Tommy could wind up a crowd and turn them loose as well as Eugene Talmadge ever could. Like Talmadge, he had the ability to "get in your shoes" and speak directly and emphatically about what mattered to a crowd.

Farther south, in another community fighting through the crisis, Alma, the grassroots movement of AAM was beginning to crank up. While Alma's group was not officially attached to any national structure or often in communication with the strike office now in situated in Campo, Colorado, it was no less effective. A farmer with a young son named T. Boy was about to fire up the farmers from the Okefenokee Swamp to the Savannah River. Tommy Carter was one of only a few Bacon County farmers who went to college in those days. To make ends meet at home, he had to attend college in the fall and winter while farming with his family in the spring and summer. When he came home, he not only farmed, but he also went into the banking business for a time. His good friend Winston Miles recalled:

He was one of a few people in our part of the country to go to college. Folks just didn't go to college around here back then. I'm not sure where he went to college, probably ABAC, then I think on to the University of Georgia, and I think I'm telling you right. I mean he was well equipped with financial situations, and why, he was in the banking business for a couple of years. Like I say, he wanted to make his mark on agriculture, and like a lot of the rest of us, he lost out. He was an inspiration to me when I was trying to borrow money, because I was young and gullible, high-dollar gambling, to whatever was going on out here with these people won't sell me a piece of land and eventually had to leave it with what I was doing, and when you get the FmHA and you owe $500,000, you just start liquidating, come back home and see what your debt left you with, you know? Tommy was a good bit older than me. I did business with him when he was in the banking business. Then he got out and went into the chicken business and farming. Then he did like the rest of us and lost a bunch of money. Tommy was a very good speaker, but he was not as aggressive or forceful as Tommy Kersey. Tommy was very forceful when making a point. He was very dramatic at times, but we've got to be dramatic sometimes when we've got a cause, you know?

3

THE FIRE STARTS
AT HURRICANE CREEK

South of Alma, Georgia, there's a section of farmland where several creeks flow together to form Hurricane Creek. One of the folks who tended about 250 acres in the area was Tommy Carter. There are many Carters in Bacon County, none of whom are kin to Jimmy and Billy—or at least willing to claim it. Bacon County was a huge producer of tobacco and hogs in the 1970s, several years prior to blueberries taking root and becoming the dominant local crop.

Tommy Carter was very well known and respected in the county. He got the idea for a tractorcade from a small news article he read in a Savannah newspaper. Midwestern farmers had been talking about holding a farmers' strike starting on December 14 if conditions didn't improve. Tommy called the AAM strike office in Colorado to request a meeting. At the Atlanta Airport, he met with some of the farmers who had started the movement to find out how to get things started. At an abandoned gas station at the crossroads of U.S. 1 and Douglas Highway, it took three meetings in three days to get everybody's attention in the county. The first meeting could have been held in a phone booth. The second one attracted only a dozen folks, but there were people standing in the yard listening through the windows at the third one. The plan was to have all the local farmers drive their tractors from their homes to the Alma Courthouse, where a rally would take place on Friday, October 28.

The tractors appeared on the streets of Alma early in the day and formed a line in a diesel-powered parade through town. There wasn't any candy throwing at this parade, but there was plenty of emotion penned up inside the tractor drivers. They pulled through town, aided by traffic control from the sheriff's department and the Georgia State Patrol. The total number of registered tractors in the first tractorcade in Georgia was 987 from eighteen counties. Farmers had come from Jeff Davis, Wayne, Pierce and other counties; the total number was estimated at over 1,100, as a few came without registering.

Tractors of every kind and color took part in the parade; Internationals, Fords, Farmalls, Allis-Chalmers and John Deeres came. There were one-row Farmalls, dual-wheeled International 1166s and 766s and huge John Deere four-wheel-drives. Many of them had posters displaying their displeasure with the president. A huge 8630 John Deere had two four-by-eight-foot plywood sheets bolted to its front tank brackets with a sign painted on both sides that read, "We need Goober Carter in Washington almost as much as a boar hog needs a set of utters [sic]." A cabbed 4230 John Deere bore several signs, including one on each side that read, "I'm a Bacon County Farmer and I'm Broke."

The rally point was the steps of the county courthouse at the corner of Twelfth and Dixon Streets. Tractors lined the streets downtown from Douglas Highway over to U.S. Highway 1. At the courthouse sat several Case tractors and a folding harrow. Well over four thousand people participated in the rally that day. Just about every person in the county was there. The crowd gathered in the street between the courthouse and the Exchange Bank across the way to hear speeches from the steps over a portable loudspeaker.

To begin the hour-long program, Tommy Carter took his turn at the podium. Then a local state representative, Bobby Wheeler, spoke. According to the *Jeff Davis Ledger*, he told the crowd, "It's not a farmer's nature to use the words *strike* and *demonstration*. It's also not the nature of farmers to be unable to pay their bills."

In the audience stood Albert and Anne Wildes. Albert held their son Alec, while Anne was only a few days away from giving birth to their second child. When the time arrived for Albert to speak, he went to the podium and laid out the situation very plainly, as recorded by the *Jeff Davis Ledger*:

> *This is a somewhat sad occasion. I think it is sad, because the great provider of plenty called the farmer has been trampled and stomped upon and lied to until he has to turn to demonstrating and striking for his plight to be noticed. The American farmer, who feeds himself and fifty-six other people, is going broke. We are the most efficient cog in the wheel of*

A John Deere 4230 bearing a sign with Bacon County misspelled waits to join the first Georgia tractorcade in Alma. *Thomas Carter.*

A 8630 John Deere sits and waits for the Alma tractorcade to start. *Thomas Carter.*

A Georgia state patrolman directs traffic in the Alma tractorcade. *Thomas Carter.*

The first Georgia farmer rally held at the Bacon County Courthouse. *Albert and Anne Wildes.*

Albert and Anne Wildes
wait for Albert's turn to
speak. *Albert and Anne Wildes.*

progress and in the economy of the United States. Before we leave this rally today, we need to recognize this. We can look back over the past and let our chests swell with pride, because we are American farmers. Truly, we have a lot to be proud of because we cannot be replaced by machines; corporate farming is not the answer. There is no way that the food and fiber necessary to keep this country turning can be produced by anyone except the family farmer. Though we may be only 3 percent of the voting body in this country, we hold the keys to the food and fiber of this country, and we hold the keys to the price of our products. This is why we can strike, and we can name our price. We cannot produce corn for $1.50 nor soybeans for $4.50 [per bushel].

The farmers are the backbone of this country. Let me ask you this question: If you were to have surgery on your back, who would you want to do it? Would you want the best surgeons and best hospitals that money could buy, or would you want some quack to begin fooling around with the thing that controls practically every part of your body? That's the situation we're in today. We've let the quacks, two-bit politicians and just general half-wits in the Department of Agriculture praise our efforts, give us a pat on the back, yet, at the same time, destroy the backbone of this country. The time has come when we must speak up for ourselves and our families, or else, we are going out of business. If a man thinks that he can invest $140 to $150 per acre necessary to produce a crop then sell that product for $1.50 and make a profit, he is a poor mathematician! Agriculture Secretary Bob Bergland made the statement to the Oklahoma farmers that if they went on strike, the banks would sell them out. It's going to take a united effort—every man with his hand to the plow and his shoulder to the wheel—to make an all-out strike successful. The banks don't want our farms. PCAs don't want our farms. Gentlemen, I think they're ready to rally behind us, but we have to take the initial step to price our products. But I sometimes wonder which would be worse, taking the chance at being sold out by trying to get what is justly ours, trying to make a way of life better for our children or just sitting back on our stools and doing nothing as we gradually go under. Unless action is taken to price our commodities, we are on the way out. We're going broke.

The average farmer in Bacon County has an investment of over $250,000 in his land and machinery, and we're classified as small farmers! Something is wrong when you have an investment of this size and still can hardly make a living. A tractor that cost $10,000 five years ago will now cost about $25,000. And I ask you, when these machines you see on the streets today are worn out, how do we replace them? Those of you who have soybeans and had them contracted may think, "Well, I'm doing alright." But what about next year's crop? It looks as if they may be about the same as the current price of $4.50 a bushel. It's not supply and demand that governs our markets anymore; it is the big agribusiness conglomerates and the reports published by the Department of Agriculture.

I want to use this illustration: in 1973, cattle prices had reached an all-time high. Housewives were boycotting the supermarkets. And the housewives were told and reports were published in all of our farm magazines—and, by the way, I feel they are knee-deep in bull—that the reason beef was so high was there were just not enough cows. Then all of a sudden, cattle prices fell to rock bottom and have stayed there four years. They dropped before a cow could even have been bred and dropped a calf. One day, we had not enough cows; the next day, we had an over-supply of cows. It doesn't make sense! It is another lie from the Department of Agriculture.

This is called the land of plenty, and truly, it has been—the land of cheap food and fiber at the expense of the American farmer. If there is a man among you who can produce corn for $1.50 per bushel and make a *profit, I wish you'd show me how. We cannot and the American farmer will not grow a crop next year and receive "Hoover Day" prices. I ask each of you to continue to work and tell all your neighbors about the strike movement. Let's not let the flame that has started in Bacon County die out. Let's let it spread through other counties and across the state and nation, and let's have rallies, tractorcades, marching in the streets and an all-out strike, if necessary, to continue in the way of life that we have chosen as our profession. I want to leave you with a story told of Sir Winston Churchill, as he often watched from his backyard as Nazi bombers hammered and battered London during World War II. Churchill would lean on his cane, grip a cigar in his teeth and repeat over and over again, "Tomorrow, we will win: the day will come when we win." On another occasion in his life, he was asked to address the boys' school at Harrow. In his speech, he emphasized ten words, "Never give in, never give in, never, never, never, never." I challenge each of you, as we work, travel and plan during these next weeks and months, to let's "never give in." Let's never give up. Because if we do, the family farm is gone.*

After the rally in Alma was over, the telephone rang at Tommy Carter's house on Hurricane Creek, requesting they help to hold rallies in other towns nearby. People from Statesboro and Waynesboro called. In Springfield, a tractorcade was held at the courthouse that contained about one hundred tractors. One of the main speakers at the rally was Albert Wildes from Alma. A phone call came in from Bulloch County, where Larry Fields was the Young Farmer president. Folks around Statesboro wanted to do the same thing the farmers in Alma had done. A meeting was held at the fairgrounds on Highway 67 on a Tuesday night. At the meeting was Statesboro's police chief Merle Clark, who helped plan how to get several thousand tractors through downtown and back home safely. The tractorcade would leave the fairgrounds and head to the courthouse down Highway 67. Businesses in downtown were asked to close from 11:00 a.m. to 3:00 p.m. in support of the farmers (and to prevent more congestion). A bus carried Bacon County farmers to the meeting, including Tommy Carter. According to the *Statesboro Herald*, he told the crowd, "How many common laborers would accept only 64 percent of their salaries? That's what we're doing when we accept 64 percent parity." Albert Wildes told the *Statesboro Herald* the rally would be called the "Northeastern Tractorcade."

A young man in Unadilla read the *Macon Telegraph*'s story about one thousand tractors on the courthouse square in little old Alma. Right after the Alma rally, there was a huge gathering of farmers and tractors at the old Unadilla gym on Thursday, November 4. The two Kansas farmers who helped start the whole Georgia movement, Gene Short and Bill Fox, were invited by Tommy Kersey to speak to the rest of the folks in Unadilla who were organizing the strike. The speakers told the crowd that commodity prices were too low. If Congress didn't act by granting full parity by December 14, farmers across the country would strike. They told the audience that if the strike worked like it should, the farmers wouldn't have to keep it up for more than a couple of weeks.

The next day, Tommy Carter, with his 766 International, and everyone from the Alma rally started toward Statesboro, making the eighty-five-mile trip in their tractors at fifteen miles per hour. They left town heading east on Highway 32 toward Rockingham. At Scuffletown Road, they turned onto State Highway 203 toward Surrency. At the K'Ville turnoff, the column passed a farmer plowing in his field. Thomas Carter, Tommy Carter's son, recalls the interaction:

> I've heard my daddy tell that story several times. The way my daddy told it was he unhooked his plow, and he told one or two of them stopped with him. He asked them what was going on, and they told him they were striking and headed to Statesboro. He said, "Let me go tell my wife and change clothes, and I'll catch up to y'all. And I'll get some fuel." He went on and unhooked his plow and tore out back towards the house. Everybody went on towards Statesboro, and I don't know if he caught everybody on the other side of Surrency or where it was. But they had all pulled over to take a break, a bunch of them. My daddy said he walked up to a bunch of them and said, "Hey! Where'd y'all say we was going, again?" He didn't even know where they were going. He just knew he was in the crowd and was going with them. My daddy would always point out that field where he was plowing; its right there where 203 runs in 121, where you take a left going to Surrency right there. There's a big field with a tall powerline going across that field.

When the line of tractors reached Glennville, it turned toward Statesboro on Highway 301. When they arrived in Claxton, the farmers were treated to a fish fry by the city and then made camp for the night. Some of the farmers got rowdy and started drinking. Things started to get out of hand. The situation was bad enough that he thought he'd made a mistake driving five hours on a tractor, only to have it go up in smoke by getting someone killed.

He put his foot down and summoned one of the support vehicle drivers to take the troublemakers home. Tommy Carter let everybody know that they were there to strike—nothing else.

The next morning, on November 5, there were so many tractors stretched down 301 that the decision was made to put tractors on both sides of the highway. After just a few minutes, the Georgia State Patrol put the brakes on the procession. According to an article in the *Statesboro Herald*, when a patrolman stopped the lead tractor, the farmer told him, "I'm paying just as many taxes on the left side of the road as the right, so I'm gonna use it for a while." Another farmer said, "We talked to the state patrol, and I told him that I'd been in the right lane all my life, and today, I was riding down the left." The state patrol led the tractors into town without many problems. But one semi-truck didn't want to cooperate. Albert Wildes, who also made the trip, recalled:

> *This guy's dead; big John Boatright was my neighbor over here. And so, we were taking both lanes of the highway going to Statesboro, and this semi decided it didn't want to pull over. Well, we went nose to nose, and I let John be in front. I had sense enough; I weighed 125 pounds. John looked like a weightlifter, but he was a farmer. He was about six foot, one inch tall and wore tight T-shirts all the time, and he just bulged with muscle, just natural. He's nose to nose with a semi, and John got out of his tractor. They had ol' butthead trucks back then. We didn't have long nose trucks. John, he stepped up on that running board and grabbed the mirror, them ol' muscles just bulging, and he swung up there into that driver's face. He said, "Get that thing off the highway!" He said, "Yessir! Yessir! Yessir!" He started trying to find him a reverse to get off the highway. He got to the edge of the road, and we went on by. I'm like a little feisty dog back there, cheering him.*

The group of local farmers met up at the local fairgrounds on Highway 67, where their tractors stayed that night with out-of-town farmers from South Carolina who were also camping out. When word got out about the number of tractors camped out in two places, the school superintendent called school off at 10:30 a.m. so the buses could beat the ten-mile-long tractorcade that was heading into town. The tractors from Alma drove down Langston Chapel Road to the fairgrounds and met up with the rest of the protesters. When the tractorcade left for the courthouse at 10:00 a.m., there were somewhere between two thousand and three thousand tractors in line, which took an hour and a half to fully clear the fairgrounds. Tractors of all sizes participated—big and little Fords, Deutzes, Allis-Chalmers, John Deeres and Cases, including a 1570 with the special Spirit of '76 factory paint job. The column drove west on Highway 67, and the first tractor appeared at the courthouse at 11:15 a.m. The farmers then circled between the courthouse and Sea Island Bank, where a podium was set up for the noon rally. Every policeman and sheriff's deputy was on traffic duty, directing the tractors through town, along with every state patrolman from the local post.

There was a huge crowd of about three thousand on hand when the speakers began. Larry Fields from the local Young Farmers spoke, as did Everett Williams, the president of the Sea Island Bank, and local farmers Neilly Scott from Leefield, Oliver Odum from Metter, Tommy Blitch from Portal and Tyson Stevens from Emanuel County. Stevens told the crowd, "We, the willing, led by the unknowing, are doing the impossible for the ungrateful. We have done so much for so long that we're expected to do the impossible for nothing." Several other farmers spoke, including two out-of-towners named Greg Suhler and Alvin Jenkins, two of the original organizers of the protest from Colorado. Jenkins was always dressed the same in every picture, in the typical attire of the time: tight denim jeans; a button-down shirt with a long collar; short, slicked-back hair; and a huge auctioneer's smile. Suhler came to town wearing his dark Buddy Holly–style glasses and a new cap that read "American Agriculture Movement." Strike news came from Suhler's speech. There was a plan being implemented to strike, starting on December 14, if the farmers didn't get the support from Washington they sought. Suhler's speech was recorded by the *Statesboro Herald*, as he informed the people of Statesboro and the rest of the state, "On December 14, we say that if we don't obtain, by matter of law, 100 percent parity for our agricultural products, we will not sell any agricultural products, we will not produce any more agricultural products and we will not buy any more. We will, in effect, shut down."

When he arrived in Statesboro for the rally, John Boatright told reporters, "I'd rather be locked up in jail fighting for my rights than sitting on my can. Even if I did plant, I'd lose my farm the way things are going." Tommy Carter informed the group that he was on strike already, "I've sold my bull, so we can't breed anymore cows. And I've moved the bull hogs away from the females. I guess I'm already on strike."

When the rally was over, the tractors left the courthouse square and went back to the fairgrounds on Highway 80. The lucky ones loaded their tractors on trailers and headed home. Others drove their tractors back; they were on the right side of the road this time, but this was not as organized as their entrance had been. Some who had tractors that were geared higher took off and left the group, while fifteen miles per hour was about all some of them could muster. When they got home, there was news from the newly organized state strike office in Unadilla: "A man named Tommy Kersey called and said they're planning to drive the tractors to Plains."

4

HAPPY THANKSGIVING, JIMMY!

A s soon as tractors were back in their sheds, plans were being made for tractorcades throughout the rest of the state. Downtown Albany witnessed a tractorcade on the same day as the Statesboro rally on November 5. The next tractorcade was seen as a practice run for future events, hitting four farming towns in a row, Reynolds, Unadilla, Perry and Hawkinsville, on November 12. The demonstration started with a rally held in Unadilla at the old high school that was attended by over two thousand people. Among the speakers was Gene Short, one of the American Agriculture Movement organizers from Plains, Kansas. He had been invited to speak by Tommy Kersey after Kersey heard him speak in the Midwest on television.

Dozens of tractors met that Friday in downtown Reynolds to kick off the tractorcade. The farmers then drove to Unadilla and camped overnight. The group headed up Highway 41 the next morning for a meeting at Perry High School. In a *Houston Home Journal* article, it was said Tommy Kersey addressed the crowd, telling them, "Now is the time for farmers to organize to demand fair treatment from the government." Then, when all the tractors were in line, the whole bunch drove, single file, down Highway 341, right past Senator Sam Nunn's house, to join farmers from across South Georgia at a Farmer Appreciation Day in Hawkinsville.

As far as the eye could see in downtown Hawkinsville, there were tractor cabs from every farm in that part of the state. Four lanes of Commerce Street were covered with tractors, parked nose to tail from Houston Street

A farmer headed to Hawkinsville on an International Harvester. The sign on the front reads, "100% Parity By Dec. 14 or Strike." *The Perry Area Historical Museum.*

A farmer headed to Hawkinsville on an International Harvester. The sign on the front reads, "We Will Lose Our ———— with No Other Way to Turn." *The Perry Area Historical Museum.*

Above: Tractors lined up for the tractorcade to Hawkinsville. *The Perry Area Historical Museum.*

Opposite, top: A view down the line of tractors ready for the tractorcade to Hawkinsville. *The Perry Area Historical Museum.*

Opposite, bottom: Tractors roll past a sign of support on their way to Hawkinsville. *The Perry Area Historical Museum.*

all the way to the old Taylor Hospital building. They came up from Wilcox County, across the river from Dodge County and along both ends of Highway 26 from Cochran to Elko. The tractorcade contained about five hundred tractors, with over one thousand farmers attending the rally on the lawn of the Pulaski County Courthouse.

According to the *Hawkinsville Dispatch*, Tommy Kersey told the crowd, "We're the strongest group in the country if we stick together on this." As quoted by the *Macon News*, he said, "What we're gonna do is this; we're gonna take the key to America's food and put it in our pockets. Then they'll have to come to us, because they'll have to." Kersey said final plans were being made to invade Plains the day after Thanksgiving as a practice run for a drive to the state capitol building on December 10. "We plan to take ten thousand tractors to Plains to show Jimmy Carter how we feel on this. Then, on Saturday,

Hawkinsville Farmer's Day Rally in November 1977. A view of Commerce Street in downtown Hawkinsville. *Pat West.*

December 10, we're going to carry as many as we can to Atlanta—straight up that interstate. We're going right on up and talking to some people about doing something about 100 percent parity." If some neighboring farms didn't cooperate, he told the crowd that they would be boycotted. But they were not going to "burn barns, shoot wives or slap mothers-in-law." Tommy Carter addressed the group and informed them that Secretary of Agriculture Robert Bergland had scheduled a meeting with farmers in Statesboro the following Wednesday, November 16. The rest of the Farmer Appreciation Day activities didn't go exactly to plan. The greased pig contest was cancelled when the pig slipped out of its pen and disappeared.

Before the Bergland meeting could take place, it got pushed back to December and passed the proposed strike date, with a change in venue to Ashburn in the afternoon and in Millen later in the evening. On November 16, a group of four hundred to five hundred farmers from all over the area met in Waynesboro and voted to support the strike. At the same time, a group of one hundred farmers in Walton County met in Monroe to support it. A Savannah rally on Saturday, November 19, didn't have much support from the local government. The rally was planned to take place at the Savannah Civic Center, but someone else was booked to use the parking lot that day. The tractorcade's starting location was changed to the Savannah State Farmers' Market on Highway 80; it then traveled to a side lot across from the civic center at the Savannah Welcome Center. The farmers' anger was stoked when they saw who bumped them out of the civic center: Herman Talmadge.

Oliver Odum, a farmer from Metter, told the *Savannah News-Press*, "I want you to tell 'em we took a back parking lot to hold our meeting, but that's the way politicians look at farmers. We took a back lot, and we took backseats and we took a back street to get here, but come December 14, tell them if Congress still hasn't done nothing, they'll come hunting us up. 'Cause they got the power and the money, but we got the food." After a delayed flight, Talmadge came over to the visitors' center and met with the farmers to make peace.

Thanksgiving Day was busy throughout South Georgia. Farmers from all over the state mounted their tractors and pointed them toward Plains for a rally that was to be held Friday on Main Street, across the railroad tracks from Billy Carter's gas station and down the street from Jimmy and Rosalyn Carter's house.

"I rode the fender of a 766 International with duals—Alma to Plains, Georgia," Thomas Carter told me. His father, Tommy Carter, was to speak the next day at the rally in downtown Plains. The trip took a long line of tractors through Douglas and Ocilla on Highway 32 to camp at the halfway point in a field near Sycamore.

I can remember my mama and Winston Mile's wife and other farmer's wives coming in trucks and cars, and we camped somewhere between Alma and Plains. We camped in tents. I remember Mama pulling up with a big fish cooker. It was a pot Daddy always had that was a black iron that he always fried fish in. I remember eating breakfast that morning and them scrambling eggs in that thing. They had another fish cooker with a big pot full of grits. There was a pile of eggs and grits, where everybody came and got a plastic plate and an orange juice to drink.

On Friday morning, the Southeast Georgia group got an early start and merged with another line of tractors; some estimates range from four thousand to ten thousand tractors. They covered both sides of Highway 280 and Hospital Street, filled the grass patches near Plains High School and the lots near the hospital and a bare field east of the city's water tank that was painted with red, white and blue stars and stripes. The tractors from Unadilla drove straight to Plains that morning. The farmers around Perry met at the Bledsoe airstrip on the Marshallville Highway at 7:30 a.m. and headed toward Plains. A large group from East Georgia camped overnight on Autry Rowland's farm near Lake Blackshear on Highway 280.

Traveling from McDonough, John Nutt, his family and other friends were rolling through Butler near the railroad tracks when his truck was hit so hard

The crowd gathers in a field east of Plains for a farmers' protest on Thanksgiving 1977. *Pat West.*

from behind, he thought he'd been hit by a train. As it turns out, he had just been rear-ended by his own Massey Ferguson 1135 and punted onto the tracks. They pulled the truck out of the way and collected the damaged equipment after the rally.

The nine-mile stretch of road from Americus to Plains was covered by a constant stream of machinery, with the first group arriving in town around 10:00 a.m. Along with the thousands of tractors came about twenty thousand farmers and their families, flooding the city from the outskirts of town all the way to Main Street and spilling over into the main highway.

The rally was held in the middle of downtown, with a flatbed semi-trailer used for a stage set underneath the red, white and blue sign that read, "Plains, Georgia Home of Jimmy Carter Our President." The banner still hangs above the Main Street storefront with "39th" added to the bottom line since Carter left office. Sitting to the right of the stage was an International Harvester 4568 that Leighton Kersey would use to lead the Atlanta tractorcade two weeks later. Highway 280 and Main Street are divided by the Savannah-Americus-Montgomery line of the railroad and a patch of grass known as Logan Park.

When the Bacon County group arrived in Plains, Tommy Carter told his son to stay put and guard the tractor.

> *My daddy handed me the keys to that tractor when he had to go speak. He told me not to move that tractor. Here I was, eleven years old. In about two minutes, here came an ambulance. I looked at Mr. Winston Miles and asked him what we were gonna do. He said, "We ain't moving them*

A farmers' tractorcade moving through downtown Plains during the Thanksgiving 1977 farmers' protest. *Jerome and Teresa Wells.*

A huge crowd gathers to listen to the speakers at the Plains rally on the day after Thanksgiving 1977. *Jerome and Teresa Wells.*

Farmers gather under the Jimmy Carter sign at the farmers' protest in November 1977. *Pat West.*

tractors." There was this ambulance, and they were trying to get all those farmers to move all their tractors, and they wouldn't do it. They had that street blocked off. I know Daddy was speaking somewhere in the city. I always heard they thought Jimmy Carter was home then. The farmers were trying to get where they could talk to him, but that didn't happen. They weren't gonna let them get close to him.

Senator Hugh Carter, the president's cousin, gave the official welcome to begin the rally, but he wasn't warmly received. An article in the *Atlanta Journal* recorded the speeches from the rally, including Senator Carter's: "I just want to tell you that Jimmy Carter understands your problem....In my opinion, he is in complete sympathy with you, just as I am." The reaction he received was not favorable or subtle.

Oliver Odum also made the trip from Metter. He spoke right after Senator Hugh Carter and told the crowd, "Senator Carter has got the cart before the horse. We don't need them. They need us to feed them....It's time to do something. If you are a farmer in the state of Georgia, you are broke whether you admit it or not. What we're going to do is shut them out of groceries and see what they do then."

The biggest reaction from the crowd in Plains came for Tommy Carter, who introduced himself as a "broke farmer from Alma." He went to great lengths to let the farmers know he was of no relation to the Carters of Plains. During his speech, he asked everyone to join the farmers' strike set to begin on December 14. He told the crowd not to buy anything or sell anything during the strike. He went on to criticize the USDA, EPA and even OSHA.

A view of the tractorcade in Plains in front of Plainview Barbeque. *Pat West.*

Tommy Kersey followed Carter and informed the crowd and the *Atlanta Journal* of the plans for the next rally on December 10 in Atlanta. "We plan to take ten thousand tractors up there and park them from one side of the city to the other in the streets....If we as American farmers don't stand up now, American life as we know it won't exist in ten years. We are here not because we want to be but because we have no alternative. We love our land, we love our life, and we have to fight for it."

During the rally, the farmers heard a new song written by George Lester. He was a regular performer at the Family Inn Lounge on Thomaston Road in Macon. The venue was later known as Scarlett Carson's. He was a retired fireman from Warner Robins performing as George Lester and Company. Lester had been watching the farmer protests on the news at home when he wrote the song. When he had it like he wanted it, he called Tommy Kersey and sent him a demo tape of the song. Kersey called him back and invited the band to perform at the rally in Plains. The song was known as "We Ain't Had Much Luck Yet."

> *When you plant your crop,*
> *You gotta wait for the seed to grow;*
> *When the crop comes up,*
> *You ain't got much to show.*
> *By the time you get to market,*
> *Through all those middlemen;*
> *Them bills they come around again.*

The crowd loved the song so much, they played it two more times that afternoon. Kersey invited the group to perform at the Fulton County Stadium rally a couple of weeks later, which they gladly accepted.

A few crop dusters flew over downtown several times, while some dustups and scuffles also occurred during the demonstrations. Then there was a huge John Deere 8430 in the middle of town that a state patrolman tried to stop before it climbed up on the steps. The driver turned the steering wheel, and as the front and rear tires pinched together, the patrolman bailed off like a skydiver. The tractor's front tires then proceeded to cultivate a "Japanese flower garden" in the downtown area. There were no survivors.

There were plenty of rumors that the Carter family was home during the rally, though news reports stated the First Family spent their first Thanksgiving in office at Camp David in Maryland. The president's brother and mother did not make an appearance in Plains either. Lillian Carter spent her time at her home south of town. The president's sister Gloria Carter Spann was in the crowd, sporting a "We Support Agriculture Strike" hat along with her husband, Walter, a local farmer.

According to the *Macon News*, Gerald Richardson told reporters after the rally, "The American consumer has got to find out where his food comes from. I've heard talk of using food supplements if the farmers strike. Well, they don't seem to know that food supplements are made from soybeans.… People have their priorities all out of order. The consumers think of their homes and cars and a big swimming pool first, when they should be thinking of their food first."

There was danger involved with the tractorcade as well. Gerald Richardson recalled: "We had a guy work for us, and this is the sad part of it. I tried to ask my wife if she knew his name. But his daddy was an old guy—had on an old pair of overalls—and he wanted to drive in it. We had a small John Deere tractor, and I think we were driving in the one in Plains. He was driving in the tractorcade and got hit by a driver and got killed. It broke the tractor in half and killed the old man. He was just wanting to participate. It's one of the saddest parts of the whole situation." The man who was killed was a retired lieutenant colonel in the U.S. Air Force. He was hit in downtown Unadilla while returning from the rally in Plains around 7:00 p.m. There was no proof of alcohol being involved, as the blood sample drawn from the other driver was destroyed at the hospital. When asked why the blood sample was destroyed, the responsible party said it was a "judgment decision." The lieutenant colonel was laid to rest at Arlington National Cemetery after he died from his injuries on December 5.

ONWARD TO ATLANTA

D ecember began with a couple of rallies and some big announcements. USDA Secretary Robert Bergland announced he would travel to meet with farmers in Ashburn and Millen on December 15. D.W. Brooks, the president of the agribusiness giant Gold Kist, based in Atlanta, also made the news with a statement about the potential strike that drew fire from the farmers. "There is no way Gold Kist can strike. We would be subject to all sorts of suits. Whatever right they want to exercise, we will support them." His comments were made at the co-op's annual meeting in Atlanta, as reported in the *Atlanta Constitution*.

Rallies were held in several cities during the first weekend in December: Tifton, Blakely, Cumming and Waynesboro. The demonstration in Tifton had a tractorcade of around four hundred tractors rolling through downtown, with a rally held in front of one of the banks. There were about four hundred tractors in downtown Waynesboro. But the biggest demonstration was held in Blakely, with about five hundred tractors attending. During the rally, the main speaker was Gerald Richardson. He was highly critical of politicians, blaming them for the farmers' current problems. As reported by the *Atlanta Journal Constitution*, he told the crowd, "Our elected officials have let us down. Just as soon as we send them to Washington, they turn against us." On Sunday, one hundred tractors circled the courthouse in Cumming and held a vote on whether to join the next week's tractorcade. It received unanimous support from the crowd.

The Georgia Department of Public Safety announced that a massive tractorcade was being planned for December 9 and 10 on the interstate highways leading into Atlanta. On the night of December 5, several Georgia State Patrol officials met with tractorcade organizers. The state patrol's tractorcade coordinator was Captain R.C. "Stock" Coleman of Eastman. The Department of Public Safety's spokesman Bill Wilson conveyed the department's concerns to the media, "This is the biggest traffic control problem the state patrol has ever faced." He recommended avoiding the interstates and the city of Atlanta while the tractorcade occurred. "Motorists must realize we're dealing with a unique situation and should be prepared to sustain some delays." Since the top speed of most farm equipment was fifteen miles per hour, the state patrol would not be enforcing the minimum speed limit of forty miles per hour. The tractors would be restricted to only the right lane. If a motorist came up and needed to get on or off the interstate, there really wasn't a clear plan in place, so they'd have to play it by ear. The state patrol said it was committing two hundred troopers, many of them riding motorcycles, to assist the farmers in the tractorcade. During the meeting, Captain Coleman requested the farmers who used tobacco to spit on the right side of their tractor during the tractorcade for the safety of the department's motorcyclists.

On December 7, Tommy Carter and three other farmers met with the governor, Vienna native George Busbee. Carter promised that the tractorcade would not cause difficulties for the public. He also told the governor that the farmers were "not trying to embarrass anyone," him included. The governor told the group that he knew enough to "paint a pretty bleak picture." He said his staff was working to open more markets overseas for the farmers and that the aid package for assisting with the summer's drought was not enough. That evening, 250 farmers met in Jefferson to finalize arrangements for the North Georgia group's tractorcade. They planned to leave Commerce at seven o'clock on Friday morning and travel down I-85 to a rally point at a hotel seven hours south. They would spend the night there before joining the protest at the capitol building on Saturday morning.

On Thursday morning, December 8, the tractorcade started up I-75 at 7:02 a.m. at

An "I Was in the Atlanta Tractorcade" button. *Billy Simpson Family.*

A John Deere 4430 driven by Pat West to the Atlanta Farmer Rally. *Pat West.*

the Georgia-Florida state line, heading north. The lead driver was Tommy Kersey's younger brother Leighton, who was driving a huge articulating International Harvester 4568 with a four-by-eight-foot red and white sign on the front that read, "Tractor Cade. This tractor sponsored by International," and flying an American flag on the left side and a Christian flag on the right. He was asked to drive straight up I-75 to Atlanta for three days and to collect everyone along the way in an orderly fashion. Right behind him was an 8430 John Deere with a four-by-eight-foot green and yellow sign on the front that read, "Tractor Cade—this tractor sponsored by John Deere," and flying an American flag on the left side and a Georgia flag on the right. The small band of about two dozen tractors arrived in Valdosta around 8:00 a.m. The group was expected to arrive in Tifton around 10:00 a.m. but didn't get there until that afternoon. When the group arrived, they collected the farmers from Albany and the surrounding areas. About an hour later, they picked up a group from Fitzgerald, Sylvester and Ocilla in Ashburn. When the line arrived in Arabi, a reporter counted 225 tractors while viewing the tractorcade from an overpass. A group from Cordele that had been waiting at the fairgrounds south of town made their way to I-75 in the shadow of the Titan missile guarding South Georgia at the Highway 280 exit. At just before 5:00 p.m., the state patrol estimated about 700 tractors arrived in Unadilla for a layover and to refuel.

Ellis Black recalled starting out twice for the rally, "I had started out gonna drive a tractor. But I had an old bareheaded [cabless] tractor, and it got colder, and I decided not to leave Lowndes County on that tractor. I turned

Right: A tractorcade led by Leighton Kersey passes under Firetower Road on I-75 in south Houston County and crawls toward Atlanta. *Richard Andel.*

Opposite: A tractorcade passes under the Highway 224 bridge in Perry near the present-day Georgia National Fairgrounds. *The Perry Area Historical Museum.*

around and took my tractor back home and got in the pickup with two other old rednecks. We drove up there in the pickup."

The tractorcades were escorted at the front by state patrol troopers in cars and motorcycles. At the rear of the line were Georgia Department of Transportation vehicles, with their amber caution lights covering the back of the line. Late Thursday afternoon, the governor held a press conference at the capitol building and declared Saturday, December 10, "Farmer Appreciation Day" in Georgia. He gave the proclamation to Tommy Kersey and asked him to share it with the farmers at the capitol rally on Saturday, because unlike Maynard Jackson, the mayor of Atlanta, he did not plan to be in attendance.

Friday morning came early for the campers in Unadilla. They needed to leave around 7:00 a.m. to meet the group coming in from the east on I-16 at the interchange in Macon. At the head of the line was a Georgia State Patrol car followed by a pickup truck just ahead of Leighton Kersey. Driving the truck was a teenage farmer from Cordele, with a CB handle given to him by Tommy Kersey himself. Carden Summers set the pace

to Atlanta and communicated with the other farmers using the call sign "ABAC," as a reference to where he was attending school at the time. Tommy Kersey answered to the handle "Farm King," or something like that. One exit north of Unadilla, at the Henderson exit, Gloria Carter Spann and her husband, Walter, joined the line on their John Deere with a weather cab and extra rear seat.

The tractorcade on I-16 contained a group that started with two tractors in Savannah on Thursday. On Friday morning, there were forty-four tractors from Dublin, Statesboro, Sylvania and Alma. The farmers from out of town spent the night along the interstate and got the line moving at 7:00 a.m. They reached Dudley at 8:00 a.m. and Allentown at 9:00 a.m. When the group appeared on the interstate at the Twiggs County line, a group from Cochran rolled down the ramp from Highway 26 and caught the attention of Twiggs County sheriff Earl Hamrick. He led the line all the way to Bibb County and radioed to the sheriff's department in Jeffersonville to send him the newest car in the fleet. He escorted the group all the way to Atlanta and back in his patrol car. Bleckley County sheriff Ed Coley also escorted the group.

Sheriff Coley recalled a conversion between Earl Hamrick and another sheriff on the radio somewhere between Macon and Atlanta. "I cannot tell you who the sheriff was talking to on the radio. But we stopped this side of Atlanta, on I-75, and some sheriff came on the radio and asked what Earl thought about it and what they averaged per acre of corn. Earl said, 'It was a slim crop. We only made twenty gallons to the acre.'"

Marvin Trice recalled the trip:

> *I remember that. We had to antifreeze the tires up 'cause it was turning cold, real cold. Of course, we ran three tractors up there into McDonough, up to the capitol and then back. We stopped at McDonough and had to leave out early that morning and head up to the capitol with two tractors up there. We rode up 112. All the people from our area went up 112 and hit I-16. We went over to I-16 for a while to Macon, where some more joined up, too, from back over toward Dooly. It got to be a real good tractorcade 'cause they escorted us, and it worked out real good. They all had to be together and not straggled out, because the tractors were going slow and had a lot of people on there, backing them up with flashing lights. Most of the tractors had flashing lights, but still. Folks weren't in as big a hurry as they are now. They can't wait. They'll turn off right in front of you.*

When the two southern groups arrived in Macon, they combined at the I-75/I-16 interchange. When Leighton Kersey arrived in Forsyth, the last tractors from I-16 were pulling onto I-75, a distance of twenty-five miles.

Thomas Carter remembers an incident between a farmer and some of the patrolmen:

I don't know if you've heard the story about a farmer from Alma. He got beat really bad by some troopers beside the highway. I was a witness to that, too. I don't remember if we were on the way to Atlanta or where, but he got accused of blocking a bridge, but he didn't do it. Another man had blocked the bridge on an 8630 four-wheel drive John Deere. He had it on his lowboy trailer, and he had parked it on a bridge. They thought he was a part of that, but he didn't block the bridge. His wife came up to try to intercede. There were four or five troopers, had him surrounded there in the side of the highway in the grass. His wife came up in there, the best of my knowledge, to try to encourage them that they had the wrong man. Things got heated, I think. One of the troopers turned around and pushed her with his hand, and she fell down in that ditch. When he did that, the farmer turned around, and he hit him. I don't know if he knocked the boy unconscious or what, but the man went down. When he did, they pulled their billy clubs out, and they beat him to a pulp. And I can remember being scared to death. I thought they were gonna beat him to death. Daddy and one or two more that were there tried to keep things under control, so to speak; they went to somebody they knew, and one or two lost their jobs. And one or two got suspended, maybe. They beat him—oh, it was bad. There was a lot of tension because the farmers were asking the troopers to do some things and the troopers were asking the farmers, and there was some tension, I remember.

The Alma farmer was driving his family's station wagon behind his father-in-law on a Massey-Ferguson 135. When the group arrived at the blocked bridge, he was blamed for cursing the state patrolmen over the CB radio. He didn't have time to explain to the lawmen that his CB had been disabled at the previous stop when his antenna was broken off the car. After his wife was handled roughly by one of the lawmen, he got tied up with five motorcycle patrolmen at the same time. The battle royale was heating up when a sheriff in the column pulled up in his patrol car, possibly either Earl Hamrick from Twiggs County or Ed Coley from Bleckley, and the whole situation dissolved. It's a good thing that things ended when they did, because charging down the shoulder of the highway was John L. Boatright, who was coming to lend a hand—and a crowbar. In the car witnessing the whole thing was the farmer's five-year-old daughter, who grew up to work for the same Georgia State Patrol.

The tractors were decorated with American, Georgian, Christian and Confederate flags. Most of the tractors had bumper stickers on them about the coming strike. Some of the tractors were covered with homemade signs that read, "Try eating your money, big shot"; "If the good Lord had intended for farmers to be broke, he wouldn't have made overalls with pockets"; "Now a Land of Plenty, Soon a Land Without Any"; and many colorful messages for the president and the USDA secretary, along with several with variations of "Crime doesn't pay, neither does farming." Chalk was used on many tractor tires to identify the farms and counties represented. Place names from every corner of the southern portion of Georgia were written on 18.4-by-38-inch rear tires, like Miller, Crisp, Colquitt and Dooly Counties, along with farm names like Bo and Pat West Farms. Some of the farmers who went to Atlanta had never been before and weren't planning to go back.

There were farmers who sent workers and relatives up the road on every tractor they had. Some farms were represented by ten or twelve tractors. If there was a cabbed tractor that was roadworthy, it was sent. To make as big a statement as possible, the biggest thing on the farm was most often sent to the protest. Some farmers took off with everything and everybody they had. Terrell Hudson from Unadilla drove a cabbed tractor to Atlanta while holding one of his daughters, and his wife, Alice, drove right behind them with their other daughter. Along the route, David West was on a school field trip in Macon because he was too young to drive a truck or a tractor. When his older brother Pat came by in his 4430, David climbed under the fence, jumped up in the cab and rode along for the rest of the protest. Dr. David West grew up to become an agriculture education teacher in Dooly County.

6

COUNTRY COMES TO TOWN

Some farmers drove their tractors all the way to their rally point, while others hauled their equipment to metro Atlanta on trailers. There were three rally points south of Atlanta on Friday evening: the Atlanta Motor Speedway parking lot in Hampton, the Simpson Farm in McDonough and the State Farmers' Market in Forest Park. The Simpson Farm was a soybean field near the corner of I-75 and Georgia Highway 20. "I'm glad this part of it is over. Sitting in a tractor for three days can get to be real old," Leighton Kersey told the *Atlanta Journal Constitution* as he stepped down from his tractor into the McDonough field. There is a Chick-fil-A at the field's original entrance, and Avalon Parkway now runs through the area where the rally was held.

When the local school board found out about the line of tractors plodding toward McDonough, it canceled school on Friday morning at 10:30 a.m. to beat the traffic problem that was heading its way at fifteen miles per hour. At 4:00 p.m. on Friday, the state patrol estimated that seven hundred tractors were at the farm or were making their way there. One of the farmers who made an appearance at Forest Park was Georgia's agriculture commissioner Tommy Irvin, driving a cableless Ford 5000. Two state senators were in the tractorcade traveling from the south, Jimmy Paulk from Fitzgerald and Ronnie Walker from McRae.

Several tractors from Hazlehurst were loaded onto a trailer and hauled to the Atlanta Motor Speedway parking lot on Friday afternoon. After the 150-mile trip, the driver got out of the truck to unload the equipment. In the cab

A truckload of Pulaski County tractors pulls into the Atlanta State Farmers' Market to stay overnight before the Atlanta Farmer Rally. *From the* Market Bulletin.

of a John Deere 4230, there was a body. A man had been drinking in town, gotten lost and climbed into the cab of the tractor to sleep. He had climbed onto the tractor after it had been loaded onto the trailer and unwittingly made the trip to Hampton. After some debate about what to do with the uninvited guest, he was awakened to be sure he was alive. Whether he made it back to Hazlehurst is unclear.

There were pockets of the state with strong representation. Groups from Unadilla, Nashville, Alma and Bainbridge sent dozens of machines and farmers. Some of the farmers sent support vehicles and vans to help get their folks to the rally point. Tractors were driven in shifts by several farmers to break the monotony. Some farmers from each county chose to stop at different rally points. Some of them choose to trailer their machines to Atlanta, while others drove straight through.

My father hauled three green tractors to McDonough: a used 2020 John Deere he had just traded an old 420 for, a neighbor's 2630 John Deere and my grandfather's new 4430 John Deere that was to be driven by my uncle. The 2020 that my father drove didn't have a rollbar or a canopy, but it did have a half-cab weather shield made of canvas and see-through plastic with a steel rod frame. The 2630 had a canopy and rollbar but no windshield. The 4430 had a SoundGard body. The tractors were hauled on a lowboy trailer with a two-ton Chevrolet day cab truck.

Sonny Stapleton remembered the trip:

I carried a John Deere tractor to McDonough and drove it to the capitol in December of '77. On the overpasses going in, there was a heap of folks on those bridges, every one of them. But what I wanted them to do was buy

54

The author's family's tractors arrive back in Milan after the Atlanta Farmer Rally on December 10, 1977. *Author's collection.*

a pack of peanuts and eat it. That's what I wanted. And drove it back to McDonough and hauled it back home. But there were some tractors on the steps of the capitol; course I didn't do that. I was out there parking mine out there where they played baseball, across the street from the capitol. I looked down and found oil coming out of my PowerLift on my tractor. But I carried it back to McDonough late that afternoon, drove it back. But I made it alright. But you talkin' about cold! Great day—it was cold!

Before the capitol rally on Saturday, Jack Frost blew into town and sliced into the temperature in the Atlanta area, with forecasts below twenty degrees in the evening on Friday and in the thirties on Saturday afternoon. While tractors were still coming in off the interstate, a rally was held in the soybean patch, attended by about eight hundred diehards. The event's speakers included Tommy Kersey, Tommy Fulford from Alamo and an auctioneer from Marietta named H.C. Thomas. According to an article in the *Atlanta Journal Constitution*, Fulford told the crowd, "The farmer has never been organized like this in history. We're going to stick together whatever it takes. We're 100 percent together for 100 percent parity." Kersey said, "We're going to win because we've got the Lord on our side. We've got all the good farmers, and we've got all the food."

The motels in town could have rented their rooms out for three or four times their normal rates, with farmers stacked in the double beds and chairs like cordwood. Nobody seemed bothered by the close quarters they shared, especially by those staying warm with the liquid fire they brought from home. One group of farmers from Houston County almost froze to death while trying to set up a tent in camp but ended up spending the night in the basement of the local McDonald's after the manager took pity on them. One farmer wasn't planning to stay in a motel. Gerald Long drove his Case tractor from Bainbridge and told the *Atlanta Journal Constitution*, "We don't need no hotel room. We drove our tractors all the way from home, and now we're going to sleep in them. So what if it's five degrees?"

Most of the farmers brought their tractors straight from the farm with their rear tires filled with water instead of air. A lot of time was spent draining the water out and adding antifreeze or calcium chloride to the water that was left to keep it from freezing. If the water froze in the tires, the tractors wouldn't be able to move until the water thawed, which would take about a week with the temperatures where they were.

Rex Bullock recalled the scene in McDonough: "I don't know how many tractors went up there—probably a thousand. And it was so cold the next morning, there was a couple hundred of them that wouldn't crank. The tractors spent the night in McDonough, and all that land where the tractors were parked, it's got something on it now."

That Saturday was the coldest day anybody who was at the rally ever remembers, and 7:00 a.m. came early. State patrolmen and farmers alike said it was the coldest they've ever experienced in their entire lives—before and after the 1977 rally. Most of the farmers from South Georgia hadn't prepared for the freeze and didn't know how to keep warm. One Telfair County farmer tried to stay warm by wrapping his cableless 3020 John Deere with rubber innertubes he'd found somewhere. Some of the farmers from North Georgia had experienced cold weather before and knew what to do. They showed the rest how to block their radiator screens with cardboard to heat up the engine. The outdoor thermometer set beside the interstate read fifteen degrees.

The tractors pulled back onto the interstate on time and crawled north to meet the group staged just south of what is now known as the I-285 bypass at the State Farmers' Market in Forest Park. The two groups blended together and continued on toward Capitol Hill. The prearranged route for the tractorcade was to exit the interstate at Capitol Avenue and circle the capitol once in a counterclockwise direction. Nobody knew how many tractors were coming in, but the estimates ranged from five thousand to twenty thousand. Every overpass from McDonough to Atlanta was full of spectators waving and cheering the farmers on. Some of the onlookers made signs of support with posterboard and bedsheets. Some of them had never seen a tractor before, much less several thousand.

Some of the first tractors to reach Capitol Hill were from Wheeler County. The mayor had given the farmers clearance to park around the capitol, so the first arrivals were parked in parallel spaces. After they locked the cabs and walked toward the area where the rally was to be held, a motorcycle cop pulled up and told the group that they would have to move their equipment. They told him to move the tractors himself as he got off his "motor scooter." As the situation began heating up, two senior policemen arrived and asked the patrolman to go run his radar up on I-85 somewhere—anywhere but Capitol Hill.

Leighton Kersey arrived with the main column at the hill around 10:00 a.m. There was a continuous line from the exit ramp near Fulton County Stadium all the way down the interstate to McDonough, twenty-six miles away. The group from the north of town blended in for a lap around the Gold Dome. When the rally began at 1:30 p.m., the last few tractors were coming off the interstate onto Capitol Avenue. To prevent an ungodly mess

Leighton Kersey pulls the tractorcade into Atlanta. This view is from the Howard Johnson Motel near Fulton County Stadium. *Pat West.*

Above: Tractors parked at Fulton County Stadium during the Atlanta Farmer Rally on Capitol Hill in Atlanta. *Jerome and Teresa Wells.*

Left: The end of the line of the Atlanta Capitol Tractorcade. Notice the GDOT trucks covering the back of the column. *From the* Market Bulletin.

Capitol Avenue from I-75 to the Atlanta Capitol is filled with tractors during the Atlanta Farmer Rally. *From the* Market Bulletin.

of hopelessly lost farmers in the middle of town, the state patrol sent the tractors around the predetermined route and back toward Fulton County Stadium, where most farmers parked and either walked back up or caught a ride to the rally.

Several urban legends have survived through the years about a farmer driving his tractor up the capitol steps. Some folks said it was a farmer from Adel. Most often, a farmer from Alma was to blame. The truth of the matter is, no fewer than eight tractors made their way up the steps and probably would have gone further if the doors hadn't been locked. Three tractors were reported to have been parked on the narrower Martin Luther King Jr. Drive steps facing in the direction of the Georgia Department of Agriculture. One of these tractors was reported to have been a John Deere 3020. Five tractors were on the steps on the Washington Street side in front of the flagpole and Tom Watson statue. Of the tractors on the steps, there appeared to be a cabbed Allis-Chalmers 7080, a cabbed Massey Ferguson 1155, a Massey Ferguson 1155 from Emanuel County and a Ford 9600, both with open canopies, rollbars and added weather brakes. The two Massey Fergusons were parked on the steps of the capitol, but their drivers were asked to move down by the Georgia State Patrol. The cabbed 1155 is the tractor that broke the capitol steps. Tom Watson's statue was in the middle of the protest, wearing an agriculture strike hat. About two dozen tractors flooded onto the capitol grounds, despite the Georgia State Patrol's best efforts to keep them out before they retreated until the rally was over. Ironically, in 1994, a statue of Jimmy Carter was erected on the capitol grounds between the two sets of steps where the tractors climbed. The Tom Watson statue was moved in 2013 to a park across the street.

Top: The tractor that broke the steps of the Atlanta Capitol. Massey-Ferguson 1155. Not owned by Ford Spinks. *Monty Spinks.*

Middle: The farmers parked their tractors on Capitol Avenue and walked to the Atlanta Farmer Rally held on the Atlanta Capitol steps. *From the* Market Bulletin.

Bottom: Tractors cover the Atlanta Capitol grounds during the farmer rally. This is a view of the west steps on Washington Street. *From the* Market Bulletin.

Thomas Carter asked me:

> *In your pictures of the capitol in Atlanta, is there a 3020 John Deere backed up on the porch of the capitol? I remember, Ernest Barber was his name; he died two years ago. He lived across the creek from me over on Radio Station Road. But Ernest backed his 3020 all the way up the capitol steps—I think all the way to the top if I remember right. My daddy and some more went up there and got him out before the police could get him and put him in a vehicle somewhere and got him took away. He had an ax handle taped to the bar where you pull yourself up on the tractor above the step up there. That's back when he was a rascal.*

Leighton Kersey parked his huge International Harvester in front of the east side of the capitol, where Tommy Kersey, Tommy Carter, Walter Stephens and several other farmers addressed the crowd. As quoted by an *Atlanta Journal Constitution* article, Kersey told the crowd, "The politicians have stopped laughing like they were when this thing started. This is the last chance for American agriculture, and we've got to do whatever is necessary." Tommy Carter told the crowd what would happen if the strike was successful, "If we have 40 percent that don't grow—or even 30 percent—it will be horrible. It will be terrible. It will bring America to its knees."

While the governor was nowhere near the capitol, Secretary of State Ben Fortson and Lieutenant Governor Zell Miller were present but did not speak. Agriculture Commissioner Tommy Irvin was not invited to speak, since he had not yet joined the protest. Atlanta mayor Maynard Jackson

The tractorcade leading tractors parked in front of the Capitol Avenue steps, where the farmer rally was held. *From the* Market Bulletin.

61

Tommy Kersey addresses the crowd at the farmer rally in Atlanta. *From the* Market Bulletin.

did address the crowd and welcomed them to town, which formed a bond between him and the American Agriculture Movement folks that remains to this day. Jerry Wright from the national AAM office in Colorado made the trip to the rally in Atlanta. He observed but did not address the crowd.

After the cold weather, the biggest complaint was the protesters were locked out of "their" state capitol building. More specifically, they were locked out of "their" state capitol restrooms. The secretary of state made it clear that the organizers didn't want any help from the state government during the protest. Since they didn't know how many protesters were coming—or what their demeanors would be—the easiest thing to do was lock the doors until Monday morning. There were several restrooms available across the street in other government buildings and churches—or behind trees, just like back home.

As the rally wrapped up at 3:00 p.m., the tractors started back down the interstate toward home. The exit was not as orderly as the entrance, with tractors sometimes passing each other, going two wide, instead of staying single file. By 4:30 p.m., the last tractors left Fulton County Stadium and were headed home, which did cause a backup in the southbound lanes for about thirty minutes.

The phone rang at the Massey-Ferguson dealer of the Tifton Tractor Company on Monday morning. The local Farm Bureau agent asked to speak with Ford Spinks, the owner, about starting a claim on damage to the capitol steps. "No, no, no. That ain't my tractor! Why do you think I need to make a claim? I don't own every Massey-Ferguson in the state!" Spinks had served as the state senator from Tift County until he was appointed to the Public Service Commission by Governor Jimmy Carter. He didn't

The first issue of the *Trooper Magazine* featured the Atlanta tractorcade and Georgia State Patrol. *Timmy Lowe, Georgia State Patrol.*

want his name associated with the damaged steps the current governor had to walk across that morning.

In the Saturday evening and Sunday editions of newspapers across the country, the farmer demonstrations dominated the headlines. No other state's demonstration came close to what Georgia's farmers had done. The estimates of between five thousand and six thousand tractors in Atlanta made this the largest demonstration of its kind in the country. The tractorcade to Atlanta was featured in the very first edition of the Georgia State Patrol's *Trooper Magazine* in January 1978. The magazine is still in circulation today.

7

THE STRIKE BEGINS AT MIDNIGHT

Everyone made it out of Atlanta safely, but it was pure pandemonium trying to get one thousand tractors loaded at the same time and leave before dark in McDonough. Some of the diehards had decided sitting in a tractor cab had gotten old. They had made their point, so more trailers appeared in metro Atlanta to haul the tractors home. One farmer who had driven his tractor up from Nashville didn't have trouble fitting under the bridges going north. But the tractor, a cabbed 4430 John Deere, was too tall on the flatbed trailer and was shortened by about five inches when it hit the first bridge it came to. He said later, "That was the most expensive trip to Atlanta I ever took." He obviously never went to the American Girl store in Atlanta.

Sunday morning came with thankful prayers for the safe return of loved ones. Tall tales were compared in the front yards of country churches all over South Georgia. Monday and Tuesday came and went as normal, except in Unadilla. The phones rang from dawn until dusk—and then some. Phone calls came in well past midnight from farmers in other states looking for advice about the impending strike. Tommy Kersey stayed with a phone to his ear, talking until his voice left him. Then he had to fly to Denver for a national meeting about the strike on Monday. Neither side was giving an inch. The national media and agribusiness leaders speculated there would be very little impact from the strike. The farmers speculated that their next move would maybe be to blockade an entire city or picket all the grocery stores in the state.

The realization was upon everyone that a strike was about to happen. Since the farmers didn't have any experience striking, they didn't know exactly what to do or how to do it. The learning curve was sharp. They had between 12:01 a.m. and 12:00 p.m. on Wednesday, December 14, to figure out how to strike and stay out of jail. Two arrests were made early that first morning in Blackshear when a feed truck refused to stop deliveries. Two strikers cut the air supply lines to the trailer, and the pair was arrested by the Georgia State Patrol for being drunk and disorderly. (If the air hoses to a trailer are cut, the brakes lock and disable the vehicle instead of turning it into an unstoppable missile with no brakes.)

At a Macon State Farmers' Market strike rally, Autry Rowland from Cordele had a stack of freshly pressed 45 records of his new song, "The American Farmer." He played in various bluegrass bands as a dobro player and decided to write a song about the farmers' strike. He brought the records with him to distribute at the strike headquarters in Unadilla. His song was recorded with the Boggy Bottom String Band and appeared on the Soybean Label. The following are excerpts from the song:

> We bought retail, sold wholesale,
> Wore ragged clothes and hung 'em on a nail,
> But if things don't change, we're soon gonna be naked.

> Cheap food's alright and fine by me,
> But tractors and fuel sure aren't free.
> And I'd sure hate to end up back plowin' a mule.

> Well, the farmers' hopes sure got high,
> Just elect Jimmy Carter and reach for the sky,
> 'Cause that ol' now he's a farmer, too.

> But Jimmy got smart, and he sold out,
> Billy sells beer on the showbiz route.
> The farmer's worse off now than when he started.

> Bad as we hate, we've got to fight,
> The time has come, we've got to strike.
> This country's got to be made to understand.

> We'll furnish the food, we'll work the land,
> We'll buy your goods, give jobs to man,
> But folks, we sure aren't gonna do it free.

Almost every business in the agricultural sections of South and Middle Georgia was closed on Wednesday, except for the Wayfarer Restaurant in Lenox. Trucks and tractors blockaded the entrances, but the owner refused to be bullied by the strike's "communist tactics." She told the *Atlanta Journal Constitution*, "I wouldn't close for anything now." Courthouses throughout the area had tractors parked in front, with signs about the strike taped to them. The courthouse in Dawson had several hundred tractors parked in front of it. The only people working in the farming towns during the early hours of the strike were police officers and pharmacists.

Picketing was a new thing for the farmers. Some thought they could drive tractors to the front entrances of food warehouses and processing plants, throw away the keys and watch a wrecker driver figure out how to remove the roadblock with no problem. As it turned out, there was a law that prevented individuals blocking the entrances to businesses. Nobody got arrested during the grace period, in which the farmers were instructed on how to legally picket by union drivers or strikers who had been taught by the Teamsters and other unions. The tractors could be placed at the entrances but could not block them. Also, the protesters could march at plant entrances but could not block them or trespass. The State Farmers' Markets had protesters at the gates, while dozens of packinghouses and warehouses had picket lines out front for weeks, protesting their use of low-priced hogs, produce and grain.

The tractor and equipment dealers knew better than to open on the first day of the strike. The feed mills and fertilizer plants stayed closed all day to avoid the wrath of the farmers. Most government offices in the rural areas were closed on December 14, except the schools. All but three livestock auction barns were closed during the first week of the strike. None of them were located south of Athens.

The packinghouses were in a pinch. They had contracts to fill with no hogs to process. The Swift plant in Moultrie was picketed for a month but got aggravated the most by farmers making deliveries of livestock to them. Long lines formed when peanut wagons from Ty Ty lined up on the yard of the plant. When the back gates were opened, only one hog would be inside the steel-sided trailers. A refrigerated truck in the line was backed into place, and when the gate was opened, only one chicken was inside. Trucks that were fully loaded were prevented from unloading for hours. The manager of the plant was not impressed. When a judge issued an order limiting the actions of the farmers in Moultrie, some of the farmers went home. The judge restricted their numbers down to a maximum of eight picketers per gate— or they'd all be picketing from the jailhouse. The manager told a crowd of farmers after a couple of days that his plant would only accept loads of at least thirty hogs. A local farmer told him that it would be easier for him to just close the plant. At that point, the manager told the farmers that he didn't need their livestock to continue operating. Of course, that news was not well received. Listening to the exchange was the Colquitt County sheriff D.H. Aldermen. In a *Tifton Gazette* article, he finally told the lead farmer, "I've had about enough of you. I'm gonna ask you to get out of here. If you don't, I'm gonna put you in jail." After reassuring the sheriff that he meant no harm, the lead farmer and his crew quickly left the lot to regroup. The plant then went back to work, using hogs mostly from Alabama.

Robbins Packing Co. in Statesboro had a picket line for several weeks, but a court order was needed to stop farmers from blocking its gates. On the first day of the strike, the sheriff of Bullock County had to get involved to prevent any violence. The Gold Kist plant in Talmo received the strike treatment the week before Christmas. All but a couple of farmers sent hogs, but with just a few hogs coming in, the plant was open but didn't process anything.

A farmer from Tift County tried to disrupt operations at Turner County Stockyard by cutting the telephone lines. He snuck around the corner, took out his pocketknife and began to cut what he thought was the right line. He got a surprise when he cut into an electrical line instead and burned his knife blade down to a smoking nub.

The next day, a judge in Athens reaffirmed the picketers' right to protest in Talmo. A judge in Lyons ruled against Piggly Wiggly Southern in Vidalia, which was seeking to have its picketers removed. The judge did limit the picketers to five per gate.

In the most violent incident reported, two chicken trucks from Claxton Poultry were shot up by armed men in a vehicle near Big Satilla Creek on U.S. Highway 1 north of Alma at about 1:00 a.m. The passenger of one truck was shot in the hip when bullets came through the cab. The other truck was stopped when its tires and radiator were shot. The GBI and local law enforcement declined to link the shooting to the protest, saying they couldn't identify the assailants. No one interviewed by the investigators knew anything about the shootings.

The one-day trip to Georgia for USDA secretary Bob Bergland turned into a two-day trip when he actually looked at a map and figured out that Ashburn and Millen were on opposite sides of the state. Bergland came down to the Turner County Elementary School gym on December 15 and found 1,200 farmers there waiting to see him. The program here was similar to the one held in Pueblo a few months previously, and it didn't seem anybody had given an inch since then. While wearing a yellow hat that read, "We Support Agricultural Strike," Bergland listened to a two-and-a-half-hour sermon inside the packed gym, delivered to him by over twenty farmers from all over the state. One farmer said that he had campaigned for Jimmy Carter in 1976 but felt he had made a mistake by voting for him.

The next day, Bergland arrived at the Jenkins County High School gym at 10:00 a.m. He delivered the news of a proposal from the Carter administration involving a new insurance plan for farmers that also covered adverse weather conditions, like the severe drought that had occurred that previous summer. It was a campaign promise from the year prior, yet the farmers came back to their original demands for higher prices. Even if an insurance policy paid for a crop at the current price, it would be useless, since the policy couldn't even cover the cost of production. After the rally in Millen, the secretary held a telephone conference with ten midwestern governors about the strike, all of whom accused the administration of pretending the farmer's strike didn't exist. They told the secretary that the government needed to mediate with the American Agriculture Movement, as other administrations had done with other industries.

Word came that the president and his family would be in Plains for the Christmas holiday. Strike leaders decided not to send every tractor in the state back to Sumter County on December 23. Less than three hundred tractors were summoned to the city for a noon rally. Tommy Kersey told the *Macon News*, "We just want enough to have the tractor movement represented. This ain't gonna be a tractorcade." In the same article, President Carter said he might consider meeting with the striking farmers, "As long as the striking farmers let the consumers know they've got a problem, that's good. But if they ever turn consumers against them, they'll be worse off than before."

The following day, at 8:00 a.m. on Christmas Eve, President Jimmy Carter welcomed four guests into his residence. Tommy Kersey, Harold Israel from nearby Smithville and two other farmers from neighboring states met with the president for about half an hour. The meeting was set up on Friday at the Carter family's peanut warehouse in Plains and was held between Kersey, Israel and one of Jimmy Carter's sons, Chip. The farmers were dressed alike in "We Support Agricultural Strike" jackets, and they gave one to the president, along with a record of Autry Rowland's newly released song. During the discussion, the president asked the farmers if they had read the farm bill in question. One of the farmers in the group, who remains anonymous, told President Carter that he had read the farm bill and basically told him it was a good substitute for toilet paper. The president's countenance fell after the remark, and the meeting slowly disintegrated after that moment. The meeting didn't change anything but did give each side an opportunity to give their opinion of the situation. Afterward, both sides had a "wait and see" attitude about the meeting. Once the meeting was over, all the farmers went back home to celebrate Christmas with their families.

8

I'VE BEEN WORKING
ON THE RAILROAD

One of the hardest things to believe was that the farmers stopped the trains. No less than six trains were stopped on December 14, the first day of the farmers' strike. Trains coming through Statesboro, Hazlehurst, Crawley, Grovania, Baxley and Marshallville were stopped by tractors, creosote posts, picket signs or buckets of axle grease. There are conflicting stories of how the train in Marshallville was stopped. One report said a tractor was parked on the tracks, while an eyewitness said it was stopped by a farmer waving a cap. For whatever reason it stopped, the train did an emergency air dump to lock the brakes, causing a coupling that connected two railcars to break. The train through Crawley, a little community on Highway 1 between Alma and Waycross, was stopped at night somehow.

The Southern Railway train in Statesboro was stopped with creosote posts and, for a while, a tractor parked on the tracks where the Central of Georgia line crossed Highway 80. Over a dozen local farmers posed for a photograph that was printed on the front page of the *Statesboro Herald* the next day. A sign on the obstacle read, "STOP, farmers on strike. Track closed." Just before 6:00 p.m., three U.S. marshals served a restraining order to the first farmer they came to, who was sitting in the seat of the tractor that was still on the tracks. He responded by kicking the paper out of the cab. After the marshals called for backup, every Statesboro policeman showed up and cleared the group. After the tractor and posts were removed, the train continued through town. The restraining order had been issued two hours earlier by U.S. district judge Alexander Lawrence.

Judge Lawrence also issued a summons for five farmers to appear in federal court in Savannah on December 24, Christmas Eve. Of the five, only one took an active part in stopping the Statesboro train. The five men had contacted the railroad earlier in the week by phone or letter, asking them not to operate the trains to honor the strike on December 14. Some of the farmers asked the railroads not to operate in their specific counties.

The Hazlehurst train story was the best one. One participant explained how it occurred:

The train was coming into Hazlehurst, bringing corn into Thomas Milling Company. At that time, Thomas Milling Company was feeding like one million chickens. So, they were bringing grain in there to them. And we knew that the engineer and the workers on that train were union. So, we just walked out there to the railroad tracks with signs that said, "Farmers on strike. Do not cross picket line." We didn't throw anything on the tracks—didn't holler at them. We just walked out there with our signs, several of us. The train got right there to the crossing where we were; they stopped. The engineer, the conductor, all those people got off and they said, "Boys, you ain't gotta worry about us." We were not an official union. They didn't know that, but they recognized that. They said, "We won't cross your picket line. Now, we'll leave this train here, and the railroad company will send some nonunion officials, and they'll drive it through. That's what's gonna happen. But it will probably be tomorrow. We'll recognize your picket line." Well, it wasn't but about two hours before we must have had about two counties' worth of people there—people that weren't farmers just raising sand, like to have a riot! It wasn't long before the U.S. marshals showed up and had heard we'd put logs on the railroad tracks and all this kinda stuff. And they got to questioning people and asking who this one was. Of course, no one would tell who anybody was. But we hadn't done any of that. If we had, you know, that's a federal offense. You can't put anything on a railroad track. But we had not done anything. We just put out a measly little ol' sign, and they stopped! So, sure enough, the next day, the nonunion guys came and drove the train on across. That was another thing that kinda helped break it. You see, a lot of farmers were in favor of the farm strike. "But I got chicken houses over here. So, that grain's got to get over here to my chickens, you know." So, then he starts wavering. He's caught between a rock and a hard place. It was like, maybe I didn't have chickens, but my brother did. It pitted families against each other. There was a lot of moving parts to that thing. The train would have been headed south because it was coming in from Lumber City. We stopped it not on Main Street but the next street over.

Some of the farmers didn't know putting objects on the tracks was a federal offense. After a visit from the U.S. marshals and a two-hour hearing in the federal courthouse in Macon, presided over by Judge Wilbur Owens Jr., several farmers were educated on the rules. During a rally at the State Farmers' Market in Macon, Tommy and Leighton Kersey were speaking to a crowd of farmers on the back of a flatbed truck with their younger brother, Wendell, in the audience. Two U.S. marshals appeared in the crowd and noticed several farmers had pitchforks in their hands. The pitchforks had signs on them that said things like, "Taylor County Farmers Will Stick Together," "How Would You Like a 40% Cut in Your *Salary*," "We Will Get the Point Across," and some less appropriate things. The farmers armed with pitchforks and clubs made it look like they were in a Frankenstein movie, and they started harassing the lawmen. As one of the marshals walked onto the stage, he was struck in the head by a Coca-Cola bottle.

While a WMAZ-13 news crew filmed the events onstage, the marshal spoke into the microphone against the booing crowd and said, "I'm the deputy United States marshal. I have no ax to grind with no one. This is a court order, summons, for Leighton Kersey, Tommy Kersey, Wendell Kersey, Gene Deloach and American Agriculture to appear in federal court tomorrow at nine o'clock." Wearing a trench coat, he produced

Rex Bullock addresses the crowd at a strike rally at the Macon State Farmers' Market on December 14, 1977. *National Archives.*

Farmers' strike signs on pitchforks at the Macon State Farmers' Market rally on December 14, 1977. *National Archives.*

the summons from a folder and tried to hand it directly to Tommy and Leighton. When he attempted to pass the summons to them, the paperwork landed on the stage.

As the marshal was nervously shuffling the papers, Leighton hollered into the microphone:

> *Come to town! We're gonna bring the whole crowd, and when we get to Macon, we are coming to Macon to stay! Macon is going to regret the day they ever served me with a subpoena. Since this thing started, I've been trying to keep down violence. I've talked—a few instances have come up. I have talked against it; I have talked to farmers to tell them we need to keep this thing as peaceful as possible. But now I've been budged as far as I am going to be budged, and I'm going to push back. It's going to push me— nobody is gonna serve me with a subpoena to bring me to court for stopping a d———— train that I didn't stop. I haven't seen a train today, but I will see the train tomorrow.*

Before the roof blew off D Shed at the Macon State Farmers' Market, Tommy Kersey escorted the lawmen back to their car and had their exit covered by the Georgia State Patrol as soon as they could disappear.

Tommy wasn't even in Georgia when the trains were stopped. He was in a meeting in Denver and appeared on *Good Morning America* first thing that morning. Wendell hadn't been able to participate in the strike or the tractorcades because he had been undergoing chemotherapy for fibromatosis,

Top: Leighton Kersey addresses the crowd at a strike rally at the Macon State Farmers' Market on December 14, 1977. *National Archives.*

Middle: A U.S. marshal delivers a subpoena to Tommy and Leighton Kersey at the Macon State Farmers' Market rally on December 14, 1977. *National Archives.*

Bottom: Tommy Kersey addresses the crowd at a strike rally at the Macon State Farmers' Market on December 14, 1977. *National Archives.*

DIST/OFFICE	DOCKET YR. NUMBER	TERMINATI MO. DAY YR.	J	N/S	O	R	R 23	DISPOS N Do Not Write	JUDGE NUMBER
53G5	77 209	12 4 7	3	890	1			6	3G06 77 209

① ② ③ | 07-11-78 | ⑤ 3G06 ⑦

I GEORGIA, SOUTHERN & FLORIDA RAILWAY COMPANY, TENNESSEE.

Vs. LEIGHTON KERSEY, WENDELL KERSEY, GENE DELOACH, and AMERICAN

TOMMY KERSEY

I Procedural Progress at Termination

1 ☒ before issue joined
2 ☐ after motion decided but before issue joined
3 ☐ Issue joined, no other court action
4 ☐ Issue joined, and after judgment of court on motion
5 ☐ Issue joined, and after pretrial conference but before trial
6 ☐ during court trial
7 ☐ during jury trial — Case
8 ☐ after court trial — terminated
9 ☐ after jury trial
0 ☐ Other (specify on reversal)

II Disposition

0 ☐ Transfer to other District
1 ☐ Remanded to state court
2 ☐ Dismissed for want of prosecution
3 ☐ Dismissed, discontinued, settled, withdrawn, etc.

Judgment on
4 ☐ Default
5 ☐ Consent
6 ☐ motion before trial
7 ☐ jury verdict
8 ☐ directed verdict (jury trial) — during or after trial
9 ☐ court trial
X ☒ Other see reverse.

III Nature of Judgment

0 ☐ No monetary award
1 ☐ $_____ 1000's only
2 ☐ $_____ and other (indicate on reverse)
3 ☐ Injunction
4 ☐ Other, foreclosure, condemnation, remand, etc.
5 ☐ Costs only

IV Judgment For:
1 ☐ Plaintiff
2 ☐ Defendant
3 ☐ Both
4 ☐ Unknown

STATUS NOTES (for court use)

DM

SHOW DATES If Applicable	Date Issue Joined	Date Pretrial Conference	Date Trial Began	Date Trial Ended

JS-6 (Rev. 1/75) Mail to: DIS, Administrative Office of the U.S. Courts, Washington, D.C. 20544

The Court granted plaintiffs an injunction enjoining defendants from interfering with the movement in interstate commerce by the railroads of any commodity.

A court case record card for case no. 77-209-Mac. *National Archives.*

a cancer that attacks soft tissue. His name rarely came up during the strike in the late '70s because of this medical issue. He struggled to save his right arm and finally conquered the disease in 1997. The order to stop harassing trains and trucks was sought by the Georgia Southern and Florida Railway Company in civil case no. 77-209-Mac.

First, the lawyer for the railroad misidentified Leighton as Tommy. The two brothers were close in age and looked similar, except Leighton wore tinted eyeglasses. The lawyer tried in vain to establish that there was a hierarchy or officers in the American Agriculture Movement. The farmers told the court that AAM was a movement, not an organization. When asked if they were officers in the movement, the defendants said their declared office was "American farmer" and said that no one had more authority than anyone else in the movement. His patience wearing thin, the lawyer moved on and tried to establish a link between the incidents in Marshallville, Baxley and Statesboro. When asked if they knew the farmers who had sent the letters to the railroad and made phone calls, some of the defendants admitted to knowing the East Georgia folks, but they did not admit to directing their actions in any way. After several attempts to pin the railroad stoppages on the Unadilla farmers, the lawyer came away empty-handed.

The judge had his turn next, explaining the situation plainly to the farmers. They had rights—but so did the railroads. He admonished them to figure out what was legal before they left the house, because pleading ignorant wasn't going to cut it. He told them the difference between picketing and trespassing. When he finished, the judgment was handed down.

> Filed order of the court enjoining all of those persons who are named as defendants in this action, enjoining all persons who identify themselves with the group known as American Agriculture in the state of Georgia, as well as their officers, agents, servants, employees and attorneys, and those persons in active concert or participation with them who receive actual notice of this order by personal service or otherwise, from in any way interfering with the movement in interstate commerce by these railroads of any commodity in any form or fashion, be it a train, a motor truck or any other instrument of moving commodities in interstate commerce.

When the judgment was read, Tommy Kersey promised the strikers would leave the trains alone.

Inside the case file was a document prepared by a U.S. marshal who collected the signatures of several farmers in Moultrie, to whom he delivered copies of the order from Judge Owens. The farmers were picketing the railroad but were not seen as trespassing on December 15.

9

MISTER FARMER GOES TO WASHINGTON, OR BOB AND EMMETT'S *EGGCELLENT* ADVENTURE

I f Plains was a circus when Jimmy Carter ran for president, it was still a circus after he left. The local newspaper, the *Plains Monitor*, was actively seeking a new owner and was purchased by Larry Flynt, the publisher of *Hustler* magazine. Being a close friend of the president, Flynt wanted to leave the newspaper business and was hoping to land a job in the Carter administration. After some joking and ribbing from Flynt in the national media about his plans for added content, he confessed that he bought the paper because he thought it was a good investment. After the purchase in January 1978, he printed an extra one hundred thousand copies for the first run under the new ownership on top of the normal circulation in a town of less than seven hundred. No reports were found about the success of the new venture. Though, much to the chagrin of fish markets and pet stores throughout the country who enjoyed the extra supply of mullet wrappers and cage liners for a few days that January, printing did get scaled back to the normal circulation within the week.

In December 1977, plans were made for every able-bodied farmer to travel to Washington, D.C., to make a statement to the government that something still had to be done about the farmers' situation. Instead of driving tractors to D.C., entire AAM county chapters chartered buses, while other farmers planned a form a "pickupcade." The first public announcement of the trip was given at a rally in Athens on January 14, 1978. About two hundred farmers drove tractors from ten surrounding counties while braving the snow and ice to attend a rally at Stegeman Coliseum on the University of Georgia's campus.

Houston County American Agriculture Movement farmers board a chartered bus to Washington, D.C., in 1978. *Richard Andel.*

Thousands of farmers from dozens of states flooded into Washington the following week. Buses were covered with signs and flags that left no doubt about what was going to happen. The Bulloch County AAM chapter took sixty-five members up the interstate to see their legislators. Dooly, Tift and Houston Counties also chartered buses. Most of the farmers who rode the buses also took their wives along.

The "pickupcade" was a sign of things to come. Hundreds of farmers from Georgia wrote their farm names and counties in chalk on the sides of their four-wheel-drive vehicles, formed a line and headed north. Pat West had a nearly new three-quarter-ton long wheelbase Chevrolet Cheyenne that needed some preventive maintenance prior to the trip.

That model truck had a front wheel bearing that was prone to wearing out. I didn't want to have to worry with it up the road, so I took and had it replaced at the Chevrolet place in Unadilla. We took off for Washington the next morning, and when we got to Buford, the wheel bearing went out again! I had to stop at the Chevrolet place up there and have another bearing put in it. When I got out of there, I knew about how far the group I was with was gonna go before stopping for the night 'cause this was way before cellphones. We drove on up and found a motel about where we figured they'd stop, and when we pulled in the lot, there the rest of the trucks were.

On January 9, a small tractorcade left Texline, Texas, and meandered across the Midwest in the direction of Washington, D.C. They arrived on January 17 at a rally point in Warrenton, Virginia, about fifty miles west of town. The farmers traveled east on January 18, the planned date of arrival of the other farmers. Leighton Kersey and seven other farmers were delayed but tried to catch up. The Virginia State Police saw the tractors and attempted to stop the group for impeding traffic. Several of the tractors stopped when they were flagged down, but Kersey continued on. The troopers then shot out one of his tractor's tires and arrested Kersey on several charges. All eight of the farmers in the group were arrested on miscellaneous charges.

When the farmers in Washington heard that Leighton Kersey had been arrested, they called every legislator they knew to try to get him out of jail. The Georgia farmers rushed to the offices of Dawson Mathis and Herman Talmadge, where the farmers pleaded for help, but they also warned that if Kersey wasn't released, they'd tear Washington to pieces. By the time the farmers left Capitol Hill and walked to the Holiday Inn nearby, Leighton Kersey was standing in the lobby.

Just being in Washington proved it wasn't enough. The first target of the farmers' wrath was the USDA building. During the evening of Thursday, January 19, the farmers were incensed that security guards wouldn't allow them inside to see Secretary Bergland. Like a bunch of greased pigs, the farmers slipped through the doors and into the secretary's waiting room. After a standoff that lasted over an hour, the crowd was convinced that Bergland was out of town. Undersecretary John White came to negotiate with them and agreed to set up a meeting the next day between some of the farmers and the secretary.

True to his word, Bob Bergland met with a group of about one hundred farmers on Capitol Hill the next day. According to a United Press International (UPI) article, he told them, "[The strike will be] a spectacular success as long as you stay within the law....Don't block highways and tear up the town. We've got something going here, but don't blow it." Supposedly in reference to the farmers forcing their way into his office the day before, he told them to do things "through the political process." Over the next few days, word came

Top: Pat West in front of his Chevrolet pickup before leaving in the "pickupcade" to Washington in January 1978. *Pat West.*

Bottom: A souvenir of "Tour of the United States Capitol" card. *Terry Sims.*

from President Carter that he would meet with the striking farmers. The White House staff asked the striking farmers for a list of possible attendees. Of the original few farmers on the list, negotiations pared the list down to three, with no AAM representatives from Georgia. Emmett Reynolds, the Georgia Farm Bureau state president, was the only Georgia farmer invited to the meeting as a representative of the USDA's peanut marketing board.

Though the meeting was pushed all the way back to Valentine's Day that year, the AAM felt their luck had changed and that maybe their protest had gotten Jimmy Carter's attention. Their hopes of a meeting alone with the president, like the one at Carter's house in December, were shattered when they found out that twenty other national agriculture groups would also be attending the meeting. Most of the other attendees, including Allan Grant from the American Farm Bureau Association, still favored the Earl Butz approach, which had little or no assistance from the federal government. The AAM representatives were given only about four minutes to speed through their demands. In the end, Jimmy Carter told the group something that has stuck with many of the AAM members to this day. According to Gerald McCathern's book *From the White House to the Hoosegow*, Carter said, "I can assure you that there will be better days ahead for those of you who can survive!" It was obvious that the president expected farmers to go out of business due to the current conditions—how many would be left was the only thing still undetermined. This came at the point that many of the AAM leaders felt something big needed to be done to sway public support or at least get their attention. A meeting was called in Caldera, Oklahoma, to decide what to do.

In the meantime, the farmers called every legislator they knew—and then all the ones they didn't know—to schedule a meeting. The legislators who had established relationships with the farmers were helpful, including Georgia's Dawson Mathis and Billy Evans. Although Herman Talmadge was a Georgia senator and the chairman of the Senate Agriculture Committee, he was sympathetic but not helpful and seemingly out of touch most of the time. Some of the farmers have suggested that Talmadge was drinking heavily in those days and was having a hard time maneuvering about the building, using an ever-present lit cigar to disguise the scent of alcohol.

In spite of the challenges Talmadge faced, he did schedule two weeks' worth of hearings on the agriculture situation. In his opening address, Talmadge told the panel that the farmers faced challenges similar to what they saw during the Great Depression. Many AAM members and supporters testified before the Senate Agriculture Committee, including Tommy Fulford and the young man whose speech started it all on the courthouse steps in Alma, Albert Wildes. At the end of the marathon of testimonies, Talmadge introduced a five-point plan to help the farmers' financial situation, including payments to farmers for acreage they did not plant with higher support prices for many of the commodities with below–production cost market prices.

Legislators from states that didn't have AAM representatives were harder to convince about the need to help America's farmers. A congressman from Pennsylvania was oblivious to the strike threat until the situation was explained to him by Jerome Wells, whose farm was located near Colquitt. Pennsylvania was not largely known as an agricultural state, but it did— and still does—produce large amounts of fossil fuels to make diesel and a brand of motor oil called Pennzoil. Mister Wells explained that if the strike continued, Pennsylvania might go broke, because farmers wouldn't be using any more diesel to plow their fields or gather their crops.

Bob and Emmett's *Egg*cellent Adventure

While thousands of AAM members were planning to invade Washington, Georgia members of the American Agriculture Movement mobilized a plan to oust Farm Bureau state president Emmett Reynolds from office. Reynolds was a farmer from Arabi who had served as president for eight years. He was also the mayor of Arabi and one of only a few farmers allowed to grow and sell Vidalia onions outside the sweet onion's traditional growing region. Mr. Reynolds grew to be hated by the strikers almost as much as Jimmy Carter was in the winter of 1977–78. Lines of communication were not regularly shared between the striking farmers and the Farm Bureau at the state level, but several AAM county offices were located inside local Farm Bureau offices. When Reynolds told everyone at the annual Farm Bureau convention in 1977 that the Farm Bureau could not support the strike because it was prohibited in its bylaws, that angered just about every farmer involved in the movement. A large percentage of farmers in the state were members of both groups and held several kinds of insurance policies with Farm Bureau. In their minds, if they went broke and couldn't pay their premiums, it would hurt the company. So, why not help get things done before everybody went broke? Still, the Farm Bureau remained neutral.

The first move was made by the Wilcox County Farm Bureau chapter, where the local AAM chapter was also located inside the Farm Bureau office in Rochelle. A letter was sent to every other Farm Bureau chapter in the state, requesting they hold a vote to remove Reynolds from office. Some chapters voted to remove him, others did not and some ignored the issue entirely. The groups that voted to remove Reynolds were Miller and McDuffie Counties, while the chapters in Crisp, Randolph, Screven and Stephens Counties supported him. The chapter in Morgan County chose not to address the issue at its meeting.

After Reynolds survived the attempted recall vote in February, the Farm Bureau state board of directors held a meeting the following month at the state office on Riverside Drive in Macon. The president and the board members invited twenty-five farmers from throughout the state to the meeting. While the meeting was held behind closed doors, another four hundred farmers showed up in the parking lot and filled the halls of the large office building. When the board confirmed its support of the president with a vote of confidence, the invited and uninvited guests became infuriated.

The next few minutes have not been easy to piece together, but in a move similar to an attack on Bob Bergland that occurred in Amarillo a few days earlier, the farmers reached in their pockets and egged the state Farm Bureau office, inside and out. Some farmers covered the exterior of the building with what were sure to be AA quality fresh eggs. Others in the building hit the switchboard at the receptionist's desk and coated Emmett Reynolds's office door. For the next few years, eggs were discovered in different places, where they had remained hidden. One egg was found three years later inside the couch cushions in the state president's office, where someone had entered with an egg in their pocket. They had intended to hit Mister Reynolds at close range but chickened out. As crazy as this situation was, no one has ever admitted to participating in the egging or even being in Bibb County that day.

Though Reynolds was told by several farmers that he needed to resign in what he understood as threatening terms, he held his ground on the strike and did not resign. An unidentified individual called Mr. Reynolds's home phone five times in one night, prompting the sheriff of Crisp County to come by and check on the family. During the back and forth with Mrs. Reynolds on the phone, the caller told her, "We can't get to Emmett, but we can get to you." From what's been said of Mrs. Reynolds, she didn't have any trouble getting to sleep that night, worrying over whoever was on the other end of the line.

The next move was again made by the Wilcox County office. They drafted five charges against the president and determined that if 10 percent of the Farm Bureaus in the state would adopt the charges, the board of directors would have to hold a recall vote. With 157 county offices, they would need approval of the charges from 16 other offices. No record exists of what happened in this latest attempt, but Emmett Reynolds remained state president until the state convention was held at Jekyll Island in November.

Reynolds learned in early October that some familiar faces would be running against him for state Farm Bureau president at the state convention. Bob Nash, a cattleman originally from Oklahoma who lived in Upson County, had run against Reynolds for state president in 1970 and lost. Harold Walker, an AAM member and Wilcox County Farm Bureau member, also ran. The election in 1977 seemed like a done deal, because everybody, except Emmett Reynolds, knew there would be a new president in December.

The Farm Bureau convention was held at Jekyll Island, where Barbara Mandrell performed "Sleeping Single in a Double Bed" but played second fiddle to the presidential election. Inside the halls, 720 delegates decided between three candidates after a fourth dropped out of the running. When the voting was completed, Nash won with 372 votes against Reynolds's 232 and Walker's 112. Reynolds went back to his Crisp County farm. Bob Nash served ten years as state Farm Bureau president.

Why the farmers in the Wilcox County Farm Bureau were so focused on getting rid of Emmett Reynolds was a mystery for some time. Since he lived and farmed so close to the Wilcox County farmers, it seemed to be a very tumultuous situation that could have been ironed out by a quick, unofficial visit by either side. In December 1977, Tommy Kersey told a group of striking farmers that Reynolds had left a message at the Unadilla office that he wanted to meet. Nothing else was reported about the Georgia Farm Bureau and AAM until the Wilcox County chapter launched its recall effort. As it turns out, there was a meeting between Emmett Reynolds, Tommy Kersey and some of the striking farmers from Wilcox County about a week after Reynolds's reported phone call. Kersey and the farmers went to Reynolds's house near Arabi one evening to discuss the strike. When the subject of the trip to Washington came up, Reynolds reportedly told the group they were unprepared and would be in over their heads on Capitol Hill. The group took it as a deep insult, and it fueled their fire to remove him until they finally succeeded almost a year later.

10

REENACTING THE ALAMO
IN McALLEN, TEXAS

While the American Agriculture Movement was in Washington, D.C., for the first time, some of the strike leaders became impatient with their progress and wanted to stir the pot. Many felt they needed a dramatic demonstration of their plight to speed up the legislative process. A meeting was held near the shores of Lake Texoma to plan their next move.

On February 21, representatives from each state organization came to a meeting in Caldera, Oklahoma. There was talk of blockading the major highways or basically laying siege to a major city with a strong agribusiness sector, like Kansas City or Omaha. They knew they didn't have the numbers, so they decided to blockade the produce trade coming over three bridges across the Rio Grande in Texas. Support from AAM was still very strong, but most of their leaders and negotiators were tied up in Washington. Less than a week after the Caldera meeting, Tommy Kersey told reporters that there would be dozens of Georgia farmers and thousands from other states protesting in Hidalgo County, Texas, on March 1. The plan was to hold three bridges across the Rio Grande for several hours to gain support for buying domestic produce instead of foreign. The AAM was protesting the importation of foreign meat and vegetables that weren't inspected or raised using the same standard as the U.S. products. Kersey told reporters that Hidalgo County was chosen because of the small number of police it had. A previous attempt to block an international bridge occurred in the much larger El Paso earlier in the year but was broken up almost immediately.

February 28 arrived and so did the farmers. Some drove their three-quarter-ton, four-by-four pickups while others landed at the airport in McAllen. Then they all checked in at the Holiday Inn in droves. There were over two hundred farmers who came to the protest, with thirty-nine from the state of Georgia. Some of the farmers were driving from home and planned to be at the protest the next day. The evening before, organizers met with the mayor of McAllen, Othal Brand, and came to an agreement about the demonstration. The farmers would be allowed to stop and inspect some of the trucks, get photographs and then open the bridge back up.

Mayor Brand was a huge produce farmer all over Texas, with almost as much acreage tended in Mexico. He not only sold fresh produce, but he also had a nationally distributed line of canned vegetables under the name Brand Foods. It seemed odd that the mayor involved himself in the protest on the bridges, since they were several miles from town. It also looked like the farmers hadn't done their homework on the mayor. Since they were going down to protest the importation of foreign produce and to investigate the possible mislabeling of foreign produce as domestic, they had a 99 percent chance of stopping a produce truck loaded with Othal Brand's very own produce. The mayor held all the cards but was playing along and was leading the AAM protesters into a violent trap.

At 7:00 a.m., the protesters arrived at the International Bridge without a produce or livestock truck in sight and very few law enforcement officers around. Mayor Brand said the trucks wouldn't start coming through until that afternoon. The farmers left the bridge, trusting the mayor's word, and planned to return when the trucks arrived. The group waited at the hotel and returned to a completely different scene after lunch.

When the farmers came back, the bridge was guarded by two countries' worth of unmarked police dressed like football players. The Mexican government had its end covered at Reynosa with federal police who weren't there a couple of hours ago. Mayor Brand was back and accompanied by the sheriff of Hidalgo County, Brig Marmolego. If McAllen's police numbers were limited, the Hidalgo County Sheriff's Department and the Texas Rangers weren't. There were four hundred policemen, deputy sheriffs and rangers, all carrying billy clubs, wearing helmets and what looked like gas masks. Parked nearby were county buses that were used to transport detainees and illegal immigrants.

One produce truck slinked onto the bridge and stopped in the middle of the road. The driver shut off the engine, took the keys and got out. A couple of Texas twosteps later, he disappeared in the crowd. The farmers looked around and assessed the situation. They realized it was now or never, so they pulled out their cameras and began snapping pictures of the load. Around that time, law enforcement gave the command to clear the highway and move onto the sidewalk. When the farmers cleared the road onto the sidewalk, the police told them to stop blocking the sidewalk. Then the order came to clear the bridge, and a melee ensued. When the fifteen-minute warning to clear the bridge came over a bullhorn, the clearing began fourteen minutes early, when more farmers appeared on the bridge. Othal Brand was expecting two thousand protesters and got only a couple hundred, but his four hundred cops didn't seem to care. Out came the billy clubs, and then tear gas popped. The force and brutality used was unimaginable and unexpected. As the farmers were attacked on the bridge, they were pushed and shoved into a bullpen then loaded onto buses and shipped to the county jail in Edinburg for processing.

When the group was attacked on the bridge, there were a few camera crews lazily expecting to take B-roll footage of farmers confronting loads of produce coming in from other countries. The journalists taking the pictures became part of the story, too. Several of them got swept into the fight, took some lumps and tasted the tear gas. But when word came down about the bridge and a jail full of farmers, every news outlet sent their best folks down to the border to cover it.

Just as the fight started, two young farmers arrived at the bridge from Wheeler County, Georgia. After attending a county AAM meeting on Tuesday night in Alamo, they drove 1,200 miles and arrived just in time to witness the action. One of the farmers told the *Macon News*, "If we'd gotten there two minutes earlier, we would have been arrested. The law enforcement officers asked the farmers to get off the road. So, they moved out of the right-of-way, onto the side. By that time, more farmers had arrived. They told the farmers they had fifteen minutes to back off the bridge, but within sixty seconds, they started shooting tear gas. The farmers did nothing out of the way. I couldn't believe it when they teargassed them."

A Screven County farmer recalled the incident: "He told a lie, the old mayor did. Ol' Othal Brand. He lied, said we could have a peaceful demonstration. When they got out there, they were surrounded by local police, the state police. They put out gas and all that, just mistreated them."

When the buses got to the jail, it took the rest of the day to process the farmers. Fingerprints and mug shots were taken; some were processed four and five times, while some weren't recorded at all. The farmers moved in and out of custody while waiting in line. Some slipped into the crowd that had gathered but got back in line because their job wasn't done yet.

The news folks weren't the only ones racing to the scene. Gerald McCathern, one of the AAM leaders from Texas, was in his Washington office when the call came. He flew down on the red-eye and touched down at McAllen Airport around the same time the Texas attorney general arrived in his private plane. John Hill was running against the incumbent governor, Dolph Briscoe, in the Democratic primary and was looking for some free airtime. The county charged the farmers with obstructing a public place, carrying a fine of $500 each. Even after the fine was cut in half, the farmers all voted to stay in jail.

The telephone rang in every AAM office in the country around the same time from inside the Hidalgo County Jail. After being overwhelmed by the new detainees, the jailers gave up trying to maintain order, so the inmates ran the jail for a while and ran up the phone bill from inside an unoccupied office. The call to arms was sounded, and everyone who wasn't already there hit the road and didn't stop until they got to the jail. There weren't direct flights to McAllen Airport in those days. Georgia farmers boarded planes in Savannah and Macon, connected in Atlanta and Houston and then caught an overgrown crop duster down to McAllen Airport. The airport at their destination was basically a drag strip surrounded by produce sheds—not exactly a hub for international travel.

There weren't enough cots at the jail, so the farmers slept in the courtyard. There wasn't enough food either. Several farmers and their wives on the outside went to town and bought plenty of blankets, bologna and bread for everybody. If there was a need inside the jail, it was taken care of by the supporters outside. It wasn't hard to deliver the goods, because the doors had been left open in the hopes the farmers would just leave, but they weren't ready to leave just yet.

Leighton Kersey arrived in town and told the crowd, "I didn't come a thousand miles just to stand in front of a jail!" As the hours passed, the crowd grew. Then a tractor appeared in the crowd and drove up to the front door of the jail. The driver threatened to drive through the building if the farmers weren't released. The attorney general had joined the negotiations, but there wasn't any give and take by either side. Then they all realized the situation was putting the crowd outside in danger. Word got out that the bridge was in danger of being leveled to stop traffic, but thankfully, that threat never materialized. When Gerald McCathern was told that every hardware store in town had sold out of ax handles, he made his final push in a desperate move to prevent any more violence. The charges would be transferred to the justice of the peace with a fee of $28.50 each. After some of the farmers had been released due to medical issues, the total fee came to a round number of $5,000. The farmers emerged from the jail smiling and covered with blankets. One farmer next to Tommy Kersey held a sign that read, "Don't farmers have civil rights?"

One of the farmers in the crowd remembered:

> *Word had got out that we had gone down and stopped the bridge. Some of the boys got arrested. There was a problem down there, and we all hopped on planes. And before it was all over with, there was quite a crowd! Then the farmers wouldn't come out of the jail. They opened the doors and begged them to come out. They said, "No! We're not leaving till all the charges are dropped." "OK, well we'll just charge you with jaywalking. That's about as low as we can go." They said, "No! we don't want to be charged with nothing."*

The next morning, farmers were back on the bridge, stopping trucks. They got one truck stopped and snapped photographs and sent it on its way. The last farmer to leave the bridge was Tommy Kersey. That day, Dolph Briscoe met with farmers to discuss the situation, but most of them had already left for home. Briscoe lost the Democratic primary later that year to John Hill, who then lost the general election to Bill Clements, a Republican riding a red wave in the election that fall. Word had it that when Othal Brand heard there would be a demonstration by AAM in his hometown, he decided that he was going to be the one who broke the movement. It would have worked if the group had just gone to jail quietly and paid the first fee handed down for a total of about $100,000. But when the farmers went to jail for no reason and everybody else flew in to help, instead of breaking them, the Texas heat bonded the group together tighter than ever.

11

WASHINGTON GOT MY GOAT

The American Agriculture Movement's invasion of Washington, D.C., was nearly two months old, and no significant legislative progress had been made. The group had met with the president once and the secretary of agriculture several times. Frustration was beginning to show through the denim hats and jackets of the farmers. On March 14, several farmers went into Maryland and attended a Tuesday night goat and livestock sale. There, they bought every goat, guinea fowl and chicken they could find and took them to the National Mall.

The next morning, as reported by *American Agriculture News*, Capitol Police reported on their radios, "Be advised. You have goats coming your way." The goats, seventy-one in all, didn't make it easy on the cops. By the end of the day, less than half of the goats had been captured. The guinea fowl and chickens were seen roosting in the trees around the Capitol into the summer. While the livestock was still on the loose, a bumper sticker was circulated around town that read, "Washington Got My Goat."

The next evening, March 16, a group of farmers gathered on the steps of the United States Department of Agriculture building near the National Mall. They had been told for several days that farmers could no longer enter the building without an appointment or a permit. Police were also standing guard at the doors, checking for permits. A march on the USDA building was loosely organized and led by Wheeler County farmer Tommy Fulford. The group had the same mindset about the USDA building that they had about the Georgia State Capitol in December. They believed the

"Washington Got My Goat—
American Agriculture" sticker.
Author's collection.

USDA building was theirs and should be open to them at any time. The secretary of agriculture had been watching things unfold and told the guards not to let the farmers in the building. Fulford and the group of about four hundred took great offense to not being allowed inside "their building" and stormed the doors. The police were outnumbered and weren't able to prevent the farmers from getting inside.

The farmers ran through the hall, straight toward Bob Bergland's office. One of the farmers' wives got pushed around by the policemen and had her honor defended by her husband; he was put in handcuffs. The group started a ruckus and demanded the farmer be released, and he was. Undersecretary John White devised a plan to thin out the crowd, so he told them the secretary would meet with one farmer from each state if the rest would leave the building. While the farmers and White negotiated, the secretary escaped the building. Many rumors and colorful stories have been told about the secretary's exit from the building, since he left without using the door. He supposedly jumped out of his office window and ran away because he feared what the group would do to him if they caught him. He didn't break anything but the sound barrier while he escaped.

Being told that the secretary had left was not what the farmers wanted to hear. The farmers knew if they left the building that night, they probably would get locked out for good. The police came and threatened to arrest everyone left in the building. Twenty-four farmers remained in Bergland's office. After a time, they were taken to the other building through the tunnel that connects the two under the street to a conference room and waited. The farmers who had vacated the building remained outside in the cold and rain to see what was going to happen. The police came again and said anyone left inside the building after 6:00 p.m. would be arrested. As the deadline came and went, the farmers stayed. After receiving clearance from the secretary for the farmers to remain in place, the policemen retreated. The farmers found themselves in a good old-fashioned sit-in until the secretary returned and agreed to meet the next day. The police told them not to leave that part of the building and not to bring in any food. After a while, a congressman from South Carolina and his wife came to visit the group. When they saw how the farmers had been treated, the two went down the street to McDonald's and bought food for the whole group. The couple dared the police to say anything about it. The farmers called it the "Bergland Hilton AAM Ag Strike Office USDA" and somehow found several open phone lines in the building that they used to call AAM offices throughout the country, news outlets and Bob Bergland's secretary to set up the meeting for the next day. Tommy Fulford told UPI over the telephone, "They don't have the guts to arrest us." At 11:00 a.m. the next day, Bob Bergland met with the farmers in the first of three meetings. He defended his actions of locking the doors, saying it was

Buttons from the Washington 1978 pickupcade. *From the Billy Simpson family, author's collection.*

done to prevent damage to the building. According to another UPI article, he told the farmers, "We do not intend to block the place. But we do not intend to let anyone tear it up. We have to take security....Occasionally, we have threats and intimidation. I don't know if it comes from nitwits or if it's for real, but I have to act responsibly." Bergland still stood by the farm bill as it was written and didn't make any promises to help. Nothing had changed since the last time he met with the farmers the month before at the White House.

While the AAM was spending time at the Bergland Hilton, Tommy Kersey and several other Georgia farmers met with Agriculture Commissioner Tommy Irvin in Atlanta, with the meeting featured on the front page of the *Market Bulletin*. When Kersey got home, he did the unthinkable. He plowed under what he told the press was eight hundred acres of wheat, rye and barley that was ready to harvest. When he was finished, he harrowed the word *strike* in a field big enough to be seen from outer space. Adam Andel, just across the line in Houston County, plowed under fifty acres of wheat, where Flat Creek PFA now sits, with his Allis-Chalmers 200. Some of their neighbors claimed they didn't plow under wheat intended to harvest, just a cover crop that had been planted to prevent erosion during the winter. But those same fields lay fallow the entire summer and fall. Kersey told the *Houston Home Journal* that twenty-three thousand acres of grain would be plowed under in Middle Georgia, along with one hundred thousand acres throughout the state.

Through the political process in Washington, progress was being made by a senator from Kansas named Bob Dole. He crafted a bill with input from farmers that paid them higher commodity prices, according to the percentage of farmland they set aside each year, in an attempt to prevent another surplus and prices bottoming out. Dole's bill was in direct competition with a bill from Herman Talmadge, and both made it out of committee and onto the Senate floor. The Dole bill won out and was sent to the House of Representatives.

Since the house majority leader was from Texas and most of the AAM leadership was from the state as well, hopes were sky high for HR 6782, the Flexible Parity Bill. The majority leader, Democrat Jim Wright from Fort Worth, brought the bill onto the floor for a vote on April 12. To the amazement of the political insiders and the delight of the farmers watching inside the Capitol, the bill passed by a voice vote. The victory was short-lived when the request for a roll-call vote was made. The bill was then defeated 268 to 150. The house majority leader had played along with the farmers

Top: Tommy Kersey, Billy Simpson and other representatives of AAM meet with Agriculture Commissioner Tommy Irvin, seated at the head of the table, in Atlanta. *From the* Market Bulletin.

Middle: Tommy Kersey addresses the media at a press conference at Georgia Department of Agriculture building in March 1978. *From the* Market Bulletin.

Bottom: U.S. representative Dawson Mathis (*the man holding the telephone*) with American Agriculture Movement farmers ready to attend a rally in Washington, D.C. *Jerome and Teresa Wells.*

Adam Andel plowing under his wheat crop during the farmer strike in the spring of 1978.
Richard Andel.

until it was time to vote and pulled his support for the bill; he knew the president was going to veto it anyway. Of the delegation from Georgia, Bo Ginn, Dawson Mathis, Ed Jenkins, Doug Barnard, Jack Brinkley, Billy Evans and John Flynt Jr. voted in favor of the bill, while Elliott Levitas, Larry McDonald and Wyche Fowler voted against it. According to the *Atlanta Constitution*, Jimmy Carter said voting down the bill was "good for the farmers of the United States, and it is very good for consumers."

Gerald McCathern, who was nominated as spokesman for the farmers, told the *Atlanta Constitution*, "We're going home and start working to put those out of office that didn't support us. Just like John Paul Jones said, 'We have just begun to fight.'…This is going to cause a lot of bankruptcies this year in rural America."

The farmers gathered on the steps of the Capitol to let out their frustration. Three months of maintaining a constant presence in Washington had come to an end in shocking defeat. About 1,500 farmers marched down Pennsylvania Avenue to the White House and let out what frustration they had left, and one old, hairy billy goat made his way over the fence and onto the White House lawn. The farmers left town dejected, knowing that if they ever came back, they'd have to be organized if they were going to get their point across.

Less than two weeks later, on April 24, over three thousand AAM members from thirty-nine states met in Oklahoma City for the first American Agriculture Movement Convention. The delegation passed twenty-six resolutions and formed a list of national priorities. The convention was chaired by national vice-president Tommy Fulford.

According to *American Agriculture News*, the five basic points of AAM were adopted: (1) 100 percent of parity for all domestic and foreign used and, or, consumed agricultural products; (2) all agricultural products produced for national and international food reserves shall be contracted at 100 percent parity; (3) creation of an entity or structure composed of agricultural producers to devise and approve policies that affect agriculture; (4) imports of all agricultural products which are domestically produced must be stopped until 100 percent parity is reached, and thereafter, imports must be limited to the amount that American producers can supply; and (5) all announcements pertaining to any agricultural producing cycle shall be made far enough in advance that the producer shall have adequate time to make needed adjustments to his operation.

One of the priorities set by the convention was for the AAM to be more visible, with members reaching out to their communities with speaking engagements and signs on their property. Just north of the entrance ramp to the southbound I-75 rest stop in Dooly County, a sign appeared soon after the defeat of the Flexible Parity Bill. On a twenty-foot-long cotton wagon in the field hung a white sign with red letters that said, "The Farmers of the State of Georgia apologize to the Farmers of this Nation for Putting J. Carter in the White House." The sign was painted at a farm shop in Pinehurst. The original sign read "Idiot" instead of "J. Carter," but they figured the sign displayed their opinion plainly enough without that sentiment.

At a meeting in May, the American Agriculture Movement in Georgia officially adopted the articles of incorporation and bylaws for its state organization under the name Georgia American Agriculture. Tommy Kersey was named state chairman, with Tommy Fulford serving as vice-chairman. Annual dues were set at fifty dollars.

Throughout 1978, Georgia members of AAM found themselves speaking to farmers in places they never knew existed, using speaking skills they never knew existed. Plus, the organizational effort to send people to different places and not the same place twice before the internet and cellphones was amazing. Nobody could recall who or where the calls came from—they just went. Tommy Kersey and Tommy Fulford both visited over half the nation's states and spoke to a different crowd of farmers almost every day. Others who worked with them were not as comfortable with public speaking in the beginning, but they found themselves on the speaking circuit as well.

Gerald Richardson recalled being pressed into action at a moment's notice:

> We were on TV over in Albany when Gil Patrick was there. I kinda got that dropped in my lap. Tommy Kersey was off somewhere—way off—speaking, and he was supposed to fly into Albany to the airport. We had another guy supposed to pick him up and take him to the TV station WALB to do the interview. Well, his plane got socked in 'cause of weather somewhere, so me and that other guy had to go on TV. We weren't planning on all that—just to get him! Well, we wound up on TV with Gil Patrick.

The farmers were able to work in a lot of places thanks to a couple of local pilots. Jimmy Johnson from Dooly County was a regular chauffeur. The trips didn't always go according to plan, said Richardson:

> Tommy Brannen, the guy I told you about, we was flying somewhere. It was at night, and we got lost. I hadn't got my solo license. I knew how to fly an airplane. But we got lost, and we were talking. He said, "Didn't you tell me you could fly?" I said, "Yeah." He said, "Well, how 'bout holding this plane in a holding pattern till I can figure out where we're at." He couldn't hold the map and watch the plane, too. We just circled around that town till we figured out where we were at.

Gerald Long traveled to Greenville, North Carolina, by plane from Bainbridge to speak to one group. Even Winston Miles made a trip out of Alma, accompanying Tommy Carter to an AAM speech. "As a matter of fact, there was a group of farmers in Booneville, Mississippi, that paid the lease on a four-seater airplane with a local boy pilot. Me, Tommy, the local boy who was a pilot and I can't remember the other gentleman, but he was from Moultrie, Georgia, and we flew to Booneville, Mississippi, with snow on the ground. But Tommy got up and inspired those farmers to get back on those clay roads on those tractors they had drove to town."

12

PLAINS, TRAINS AND TRACTORCADES

The American Agriculture Movement continued to hold rallies where Georgia farmers were the keynote speakers throughout the summer. The AAM had a booth at the very first Sunbelt Agriculture Exposition ever held. The farm show was previously held in the spring on the ABAC campus near Tifton and called the Farm Power and Recreation Show. The booth was manned by several Georgia farmers who spent their time explaining the movement to other farmers from around the Southeast. Rallies and parades started back up around the holidays.

On Thursday, November 9, the first recorded tractorcade in Georgia since the D.C. trip was held in Unadilla, followed by a rally. On Wednesday, December 13, the Telfair and Wheeler County chapters held a Farmers Appreciation Day in McRae. A tractorcade started the day off, traveling through downtown, with over one hundred tractors participating. The tractorcade wound through town to the Jaycee building at the fairgrounds. Speakers included Agriculture Commissioner Tommy Irvin, State Senator Ronnie Walker, AAM national office representative Alvin Jenkins and aides from Representative Billy Evans's and Senator Sam Nunn's offices. The Telfair County High School band played for the three hundred attendees while they ate barbeque for lunch. The rally was broadcast by the local radio station, WDAX AM 1410.

Thanksgiving was relatively quiet around Plains in 1978. The farmers had learned their lesson the year before, when ten thousand tractors drove from all over the state to protest in front of an empty Carter residence. The president and his family stayed near Washington again for Thanksgiving.

Left: The American Agriculture Movement booth at the first ever Sunbelt Agricultural Exposition at Spence Field in Moultrie. *Richard Andel.*

Opposite: AAM farmers block downtown near the Plains depot during a Christmas protest prior to President Carter's arrival on Christmas Day 1978. *Jerome and Teresa Wells.*

On Monday, December 18, Police Chief Billy McClung announced that two protest rallies would be held in Plains over the holiday. On Friday, December 22, the AAM was planning a tractorcade through downtown Plains prior to the arrival of the president and his family, which the police and the president's staff hoped would be cleared out by the time President Carter arrived. On Saturday, a group of Taiwanese protesters rallied to show their opposition to the president's reestablishment of communications with the Chinese and his excommunication of Taiwan.

The farmers didn't send everyone to Plains in 1978. This time, they were organized and ready, with just about 250 tractors placed at every stop sign in town. The tractorcade permit was set to expire at 5:00 p.m., with the president scheduled to arrive at 9:00 p.m. If Chief McClung thought the farmers were going to move out of the way so Jimmy Carter could get home to celebrate Christmas in peace, he was about to be very disappointed—and very busy.

On December 22, the farmers gathered in downtown around noon at a stage made from a flatbed trailer at the same location it occupied in 1977, in front of the storefronts on Main Street. As if emotions weren't high enough, the group learned of a terrible accident that had occurred early that morning. Two planeloads of farmers from Qulin, Missouri,

were traveling to Plains to join the protest. Around 5:30 a.m., the two planes took off. One of the planes began having trouble as soon as it was airborne from an undetected cracked propeller. The pilot, Keith Sentell, could barely make out where the ground was in the dim light but spotted a field ahead that looked safe to set the wounded plane down in. After the plane was airborne for only ten minutes, Sentell attempted to set it down and clipped a couple of trees at the edge of the field. Contact with the trees caused the plane to hit the ground nose first. When communication between the two planes was lost, the other plane circled the area, searching for the aircraft. The farmers decided to land and look for the plane in their vehicles.

The crash site was found about two hours later. When they could do no more for their friends, the surviving farmers decided to honor them by completing their trip to Plains. The farmers killed in the crash included the pilot, Keith Sentell, and his brother, Randy Sentell; Walter Lee Webb Jr.; and Terry Eugene Thomas, all from Qulin. When news of the crash made it to Georgia, the protesters all wore black armbands to honor their fallen friends. The farmers who completed the trip were all from Missouri, including the pilot, James Flanigan from White Oak, Wayne Cryts from Puxeco and Randy Nations and Ronny Maddox, both from Campbell.

The rally on Main Street went ahead as scheduled but with a very somber tone. There were speeches given, but none were made by Hugh Carter this time. Country bands played, and dancers performed on the flatbed stage. A roar went up from the crowd when the four men from Qulin, Missouri, came onstage. According to the *Macon Telegraph*, Randy Maddox from Campbell, Missouri, asked them, "If we'd had presidents like this for the last one hundred years, where would we be now?"

Tractors were parked along every street and highway around town, while the clock ticked down to 5:00 p.m. As the clock struck the deadline, there were tractors of all shapes and sizes in the middle of the road. The state patrol commander and Plains police chief knew the president was on his way but would not arrive for a couple of hours. They moved the deadline to 6:00 p.m. in an attempt to ease tensions. In the crowd, there were several John Deere 8630s, cabbed, high-horsepower, articulating tractors with four or eight huge tires. Gerald Richardson drove one 8630 with a bulldozer blade on the front to Plains that day. He pulled the tractor into the center of Highway 280, dropped the blade, shut off the engine, took out the key, locked the door and singlehandedly locked down the main highway through town. Another 8630 came from Main Street, across the railroad tracks and stopped in front of Billy Carter's gas station. The driver shut it down, got off the steps, removed the glass fuel filters attached to the engine block, put them in his pocket with the key and disappeared. A farmer from Screven County sat on his cabless 285 Massey-Ferguson tractor at intersection of Highways 45 and 280, daring the state patrol to pull him off of it.

Six o'clock came quickly in Plains, marked by the evening's failing light and the sight of several dozen state patrolmen putting on riot gear in plain sight of the farmers. Helmets and billy clubs were issued as the order to clear the highway was given. The sight of law enforcement officers climbing onto the farmers' equipment and the use of wreckers to clear the highway touched off the situation. But the farmers didn't shy away from contact, with several being hit. Four men were arrested for refusing to obey a law enforcement officer. Two of the men, Wayne Cryts and Ronny Maddox, had been on the plane from Missouri that morning. A young farmer from Mitchell County was arrested but was sent to the hospital after being injured by a blow to the head from a billy club. The last man arrested was the farmer who sat on his 285 Massey-Ferguson in the middle of Highways 280 and 45, probably wishing he'd brought a tractor with a cab on it to Plains.

The City of Plains Police Station is located directly across the street from Billy Carter's place. For some reason, the three uninjured farmers spent two and a half hours in the back of a state patrol car with a front-row seat to the action. Tommy Kersey and Tommy Fulford were the lead negotiators with Police Chief McClung, Georgia State Patrol captain Stewart McGlaun and Sumter County sheriff Randy Howard. The sheriff offered to release the men if the other farmers would leave and take their tractors. That suggestion was quickly shouted down. As the situation started to get out of hand, one of the 8630s cranked up to move off the highway. Everyone watched as the tractor left the roadway and parked on the railroad tracks. Again, the driver got out, locked the door, disabled the machine and disappeared. The farmers promised not to move the tractor until their friends were released. The sheriff contacted the railroad office and was told there was a train headed to Montgomery from Americus, headed for the middle of Plains. Sheriff Howard told them about the protest and that there was a large, disabled tractor blocking the tracks. The train pulled to a stop in front of the Carter Warehouse, where it waited for the negotiations to conclude. While the train sat still, the sheriff released the prisoners. For the rest of their time in Plains, the farmers carried ax handles on their tractors.

Aside from the radios in the law enforcement officers' cars, the only contact the group had with the outside world was a single payphone located in a diner on Highway 280. Early in the day, several phone calls were made from the booth. As the action was heating up, a plainclothes "repairman" was seen working on something behind the phone. It was rendered useless by the stranger until the president left town, preventing anyone from calling in reinforcements.

Air Force One landed first at Dobbins Air Force Base for the president to visit Crawford W. Long Memorial Hospital. His first granddaughter had been born to Jack and Judy Carter, the president's oldest son, earlier in the week. After taking off again, the Carters landed at the Fort Benning Airfield near Columbus and were greeted by friends and serenaded by the Columbus High School band. The president and his family rode the presidential helicopter, *Marine One*, from the base to an airstrip north of town on Highway 45 called Peterson Field. The president's limousine took him to the Carter residence but had to go the back way on Paschal Street. The road in front of the house, Highway 280, was blocked by a bunch of striking Georgia farmers.

The group of farmers gathered in downtown were not close enough to see the president's house. They were at least a half mile from it. Some of the wilder-spirited farmers suggested they take the tractors straight down the lane to the Carters' front door. He surmised, "They can't get us all!"

The eagle statue that accidently fell in downtown Plains on the night of December 23, 1978. *Author's collection.*

Another farmer told him no. "They've got stuff down there that will stop a tank. What do you think they would do to a tractor?"

The occupation of downtown Plains continued throughout the night, as several farmers and their tractors sat in the street downtown. At some point after midnight, an eagle statue that had been given to the president and then displayed in downtown fell over by accident. No one saw what happened to it; it just fell. The captain of the Georgia State Patrol attempted to pry a confession from some of the farmers, who were uncooperative in his investigation. The eagle was stood back up and hasn't fallen over since.

As the morning broke, the farmers were still there, even though their parade permit had expired fourteen hours earlier. At noon, the Taiwanese protesters showed up to protest in downtown. Instead of causing any trouble, the farmers left and gave this new group of protesters their chance to be heard. The farmers were allowed to leave their tractors beside Highway 280 until after Christmas was over.

On Christmas Eve, two thousand people came to Qulin, Missouri, to pay their respects to the fallen farmers. Each farmer had already planned to attend the tractorcade to D.C. in January. The tractor each farmer was going to drive on the trip was at the Two Rivers Junior High School, draped with black cloth. Two representatives from each of the twenty-five states participating in AAM attended the funeral.

The presidential family left Plains after Christmas and headed back to D.C. Jimmy Carter was never in contact with the protesters. No backchannel communications were shared. No plans to meet with him were made. The protesters only wanted to show the president that the farmers were still around, and they still had problems. They were all busy planning something big. If Jimmy Carter didn't pay them any attention at his home in Plains, maybe he'd pay attention to them after they drove their tractors all the way to the White House.

13

PLANNING A TRACTORCADE
TO WASHINGTON

I n early October 1978, plans were being made for a tractorcade to Washington. In Lubbock, Texas, the national AAM leaders were trying to figure out how to funnel tractors from around the United States into Washington and arrive there at the same time. In 1978, there was no GPS available to civilians—no Google Maps and no internet. The planners used matchsticks to calculate how far a tractor could travel in one day and how many days it would take for tractors on each route to reach Washington. The plan called for the farmers to enter Washington at the worst possible time, Monday morning at rush hour. The routes were calculated, and the plan was to arrive in Washington on February 5, 1979.

Eight main departure points on major highways in the Midwest were chosen and timed based on where the tractors would arrive at several campgrounds in Virginia and Maryland the week before their planned invasion the following Monday. The starting points were located in Houston on I-59, Abilene on I-20 and Amarillo on I-40 in Texas; Topeka, Kansas, on I-70; Lamar, Colorado, on U.S. Highway 400; Grand Island, Nebraska, on I-80; Mitchell, South Dakota, on I-90; and Fargo, North Dakota, on I-94. Farmers from farther out west trucked their equipment to their nearest departure point by trailer. Each leg had a "wagon master" at the head of the column, with Gerald McCathern serving as national wagon master while also leading the leg on I-40 out of Amarillo. The wagon master for the southernmost leg that would lead the Georgia farmers into D.C. was Mell "Mad Dog" Cherry, starting out of Houston.

All roads lead to Washington, D.C., in 1979! Instructions for the tractorcade to Washington from the AAM office in Unadilla. *Richard Andel.*

A map of the planned routes taken by the tractorcade to Washington in 1979. *Richard Andel.*

The tractorcade's original departure date was January 22, with the arrival in D.C. scheduled for February 12. When the Senate and Congress set their calendars in early January, they arranged a weeklong adjournment starting the day the Tractorcade planned to arrive. Word of this reached the national headquarters, and the departure date was moved up an entire week, to Monday, January 15. The tractors would travel the interstate system the entire time at fifteen miles per hour for an average of one hundred miles per day for sixteen days, plus two Sundays for rest.

The locations of suggested checkpoints and setups were distributed to all participants a couple of weeks prior to departure. The checklist and final instructions were mailed out and also printed in the *American Agriculture News* in early January. The tractors were to be serviced with all their oil and filters changed. Batteries and alternators needed to be checked and changed if necessary. All weights were to be removed and water drained from the tires. The rear tires were to be turned backward and inflated to thirty-five pounds per square inch, with the front tires inflated to forty pounds per square inch to reduce wear. All wipers, lights and flashers were to be checked.

The tractors, support vehicles and campers were to travel with others from their local communities. Each state had its own system of numbering its equipment to stay lined up. As with the tractorcade to Atlanta in 1977, the counties and states of origin were written in chalk on the tractors' tires and hoods. Signs and flags were used liberally. The American flag, AAM flag, state flags and Christian flag were on most every tractor. Plenty of support vehicles were farm trucks driven by wives or relatives. There was at least one camper pulled by a family's tractor or truck. Suggested to be among the support vehicles were oil and enough fuel tanks to fill each tractor in the group, joint grease and wheel bearing grease, paper towels, windshield cleaner, hoses, wiper blades, belts, antifreeze, tools, battery chargers, flashlights, batteries, CBs, fuses, light bulbs, tape, jacks, torches, welders, air compressors, tire patches, et cetera. The suggested supplies in each tractor included shoes, locks, chains, a thermos, shovels, blankets and, of course, duct tape. Each tractor and truck had to have a CB and a VHF radio in its support vehicle. Channel 14 was the designated channel the wagon master used to communicate with the column. Every morning, fuel that was donated by local farmers or fuel distributors was hauled in on tank trucks. Each group's support vehicle got in line to fill holding tanks to distribute to its group. No fuel was bought by the tractors' drivers after their initial fill-up when they left home.

On Monday, January 15, 1979, at 8:00 a.m. CST, Gerald McCathern cranked up an International 1486 in Bushland, Texas, and began the tractorcade to Washington; 210 tractors and trucks pulled onto Interstate 40 just west of the Cadillac Ranch and headed toward Amarillo; 110 tractors and trucks left Abilene, Texas, around the same time; 8 vehicles rolled out of Bismarck, North Dakota, in negative-twenty-five-degree weather.

By Wednesday, January 17, the I-20 group that started in Abilene had traveled through Dallas–Fort Worth and were catching their breaths in Canton, Texas. Gerald McCathern's group on Interstate 40 had passed through Oklahoma City and was resting in Okemah, about 100 miles west of Fort Smith, Arkansas. Thirty-five tractors and trucks left WaKeeney, Kansas, about 240 miles west of Topeka, on slick, icy roads but made it halfway to Topeka before sundown. The groups in North Platte, Nebraska, and Mitchell, South Dakota, left on January 17. The groups in North and South Dakota were facing a blizzard that was coming in from Canada; it forced them to stop in Luverne, Minnesota, before detouring to the south and traveling with the Nebraska group.

On Saturday, January 20, the Abilene group crossed the Ouachita River into Monroe, Louisiana, where they spent the weekend. On Monday, the group met with Mississippi's governor and agriculture commissioner, while some of the farmers addressed the state senate and house of representatives. Governor Cliff Finch invited the group to the governor's mansion to spend the night if they needed a place to stay. When the Kansas group passed through Kansas City, Missouri, they picked up a farmer whose wife was due to give birth in about a month. Their baby girl came ahead of time—the following day. She was appropriately named Parity. The Missouri State Police didn't allow the tractors on the section of I-70 between Kansas City and Saint Louis and had the group divert onto U.S. Highway 50 to cross the state. The tractors weren't slowed down much by the detour because it paralleled I-70 and connected Kansas City and Saint Louis as well.

The trip had gone according to plan until the Abilene group made the mistake of camping somewhere near Tuscaloosa on January 23. When the group woke up the next morning, every AAM flag on each vehicle had been stolen. Their last overnight stop before linking up with the Georgia farmers was at Talladega Superspeedway in Eastaboga, Alabama, on Wednesday. The Kansas group stopped about seventy miles east of Saint Louis, Missouri, in Vandalia, Illinois, because of ice. The three northern groups had combined to try to outflank the blizzard but ran out of luck in Galesburg, Illinois. They were snowed in and delayed about fifty miles west of Peoria.

When Gerald McCathern's Amarillo group arrived in Nashville, Tennessee, Houston County farmer Adam Andel's son Richard was working there for Detroit Diesel. He went to see the tractorcade when it stopped for the night at the Nashville Fairgrounds, south of town. In the crowd, he saw an antique propane-powered John Deere G with canvas sides. A farmer named Don Kimbrell drove that tricycle front end, open-cabbed tractor from Happy, Texas, all the way to Washington.

The Georgia group's original departure point was Lake City, Florida, where the farmers left early on January 22 and headed north on I-75. They arrived in Valdosta, picked up several South Georgia farmers, camped and departed the next day. The caravan arrived at Unadilla on January 23 and camped next to the interstate until morning. Most of the South Georgia group chose to haul their equipment to Unadilla and depart with Tommy Kersey, including Gerald Long in a Case 1570; Adam Andel inside his Allis-Chalmers 200, followed by Talmadge Tomlinson in a long-wheelbase Ford pulling a twenty-foot-long camper; and the Wellses from Miller County, driving a John Deere 4230 and a Winnebago. On January

Adam Andel drives his Allis-Chalmers 200, pulling a camper, followed by T.E. Tomlinson on I-75 near Perry in the 1979 Washington tractorcade. *Richard Andel.*

24, the group left Unadilla, with Tommy Kersey in the lead tractor. The line had just gotten up to speed when Kersey radioed his wife, saying that he'd left his dinner at the house. His wife radioed back that she would meet him at the next exit up the road with his food. The Georgia group was scheduled to meet the group from Houston on I-20 at Atlanta–Fulton County Stadium on January 25.

Tommy Fulford led a group out of Alamo toward Dublin and up I-16. They spent the night in the Macon Coliseum parking lot before joining the main group at the I-16/I-75 junction the next morning. In Dublin, Fulford opened the door of a brand-new John Deere 4240 that had been donated to him to drive to D.C. by the John Deere dealership in Douglas. He let a reporter ride in the tractor cab all the way to Macon for an interview. Many of the tractors that were driven to Washington were donated by local equipment dealers who had a lot riding on the outcome of the tractorcade as well. Ms. Mitt, Herman Talmadge's mother, reportedly sponsored a 4640 from McRae that also made the trip to D.C.

There were numerous other routes and departure points used to filter in tractors from areas not in the direct path of the planned approach, such as the I-95 leg that brought up the East Georgia farmers. A group of farmers from Sylvania joined north of Savannah sometime around January 24 and planned to meet the main group in North Carolina in a couple of days.

A thirty-mile-long line of tractors and trucks from the west appeared on I-20, crossing the state line on January 25. Large red and green equipment with Texas and Christian flags were flying on every vehicle. After they left Birmingham, they had to stop in the emergency lane to repair a tire on David Senter's tractor at the Highway 6 exit, where Six Flags now sits. The group met with national and Atlanta news crews before rolling into Atlanta at 3:30 p.m. and turning into the parking lot at Fulton County Stadium to meet the South Georgia convoy from I-75. After a 6:30 p.m. rally at the stadium, the farmers turned in to spend the night.

At 7:00 a.m. on Friday, the tractors were rolling again and took I-85 north with an escort to the state line by the Georgia State Patrol. Before leaving town, a farmer from Arizona picked up a passenger at Fulton County Stadium, reporter Charles Seabrook from the *Atlanta Journal*. The South Carolina State Police met the farmers at the state line near Fair Play and led them up the first exit ramp they came to. Some of the tractors at the head of the line smelled a rat and thought they were being led off the interstate and away from their destination. After Tommy Kersey worked his way through the group, everybody calmed down and found out the patrolman was leading them to their campsite for the night near Townville, several miles off the interstate.

On Saturday morning, the tractors were again rolling toward Charlotte, North Carolina, where several hundred trucks and tractors spent the weekend at the Charlotte Fairgrounds, home of Charlotte Motor Speedway. A reporter counted approximately 260 tractors and 240 support vehicles at the fairgrounds. The tractorcade, no matter where it was, didn't travel on Sundays. The group continued north on Monday and spent the next night north of Durham. There wasn't a campsite in Durham to stop in, just a neighborhood where the tractors slipped in off the highway and rested for a spell.

Plans were made to spend Tuesday night, January 30, at an army base or park near Petersburg, Virginia, the site of one of the last battles of the Civil War. Whether the government or a private landowner made the call, the agreement fell through. The tractorcade exited the interstate and camped on the shoulder of U.S. Highway 1, which parallels the interstate at Dinwiddie. The call came from "Mad Dog" Cherry to park a tractor behind each camper in case a car strayed off its path. Many anxious moments passed that night.

Trucks lined up to refuel at the Charlotte Fairgrounds in North Carolina during the 1979 Washington tractorcade. *Richard Andel.*

Wednesday morning could not come soon enough. The column cranked up, warmed up and got in gear for the final leg of the journey. A miscommunication at the toll plaza on I-95 caused a preview of what a pile of stalled tractors can do in traffic. The head of the Virginia Department of Transportation threatened to send a bill to the American Agriculture Movement for all the tractors that passed through the toll. Until the situation got straightened out, a tractor sat and blocked traffic at every toll booth.

By Wednesday evening, the I-20/I-85 group was camped at Pohick Campground near Alexandria, Virginia, on the west bank of the Potomac River. Another group of about one thousand farmers was camped nearby at Bull Run Regional Park. There, they all sat and waited for the rest of the tractorcades from out west to arrive, including the group that had been delayed by several snowstorms. Gerald McCathern told the group that no one was to cross the bridge into D.C. until Monday morning. So, they all waited.

Pohick Campground filled up quickly. There were tractors all over Northern Virginia and Maryland. On the east side of D.C., tractors sat

Top: Jerome Wells exits the cab of his John Deere tractor after a long drive toward Washington, D.C. *Jerome and Teresa Wells.*

Bottom: Tractors line up to leave Pohick Campground in Virginia on February 5, 1979, and prepare to enter Washington during rush hour. *Richard Andel.*

out the weekend at RFK Stadium, where the Washington Redskins played. Tractors were parked at farms that had sent word they could hold fifty or sixty campers, but most of the time, one hundred showed up.

While the Tractorcade was headed east to Washington, D.C., the senior senator from Georgia and chairman of the Senate Agriculture Committee, Herman Talmadge, was headed west to California. After several years of battling alcoholism, he bravely checked himself into the Walter Reid Naval Hospital in Maryland and was then transferred to the Betty Ford Clinic. Two years after presiding over the Watergate hearings, Talmadge lost an adult son, who drowned while swimming in Lake Lanier. Soon after that, the senator was checked in at Walter Reid but left after only three days. Soon after that came a nasty and very public divorce from his very popular and well-liked wife, Betty. At the start of the 1979 legislative session, he was scrutinized by the Senate for misappropriating campaign funds. He quickly blamed the discrepancy on an aide who had been hired to work with his 1974 Senate campaign.

Talmadge admitted to appearing on the Senate floor while intoxicated only once while escorting newly elected senator Sam Nunn to his seat in November 1972. In January 1979, after being confronted by his son Gene, he removed himself from the powerful seat he had occupied for two decades to become a patient in a rehabilitation clinic with no timetable for his return. The vice-chairman of the Agriculture Committee at the time, Jesse Helms of South Carolina, would run his committee until he returned.

14

THE TRACTORCADE TO NOWHERE

A t 4:00 a.m. on February 5, 1979, ten thousand farmers cranked up their tractors, trucks and campers and filed out of their campgrounds toward one destination: the USDA building in Washington, D.C. The farmers had a rally permit at the National Mall in front of the Capitol on Monday and Tuesday, but their paperwork didn't mention any tractors. Several columns of farm equipment crawled along the highways like ants and crossed the Potomac River on every bridge they could find. The group that camped at Bull Run Regional Park took I-66 earlier than everybody else to make up the thirty-mile distance and arrive at the Francis Scott Key Bridge by 7:00 a.m. From there, they crossed the river and took the Whitehurst Freeway. Then they turned south to meet the other farmers gathering on the south side of the National Mall.

The I-20/I-85 farmers who stayed at Pohick Campground were already on the Fourteenth Street Bridge at about 5:00 a.m. Also designated the I-395 bridge, that route runs behind the Jefferson Memorial and Tidal Basin, then flows directly into downtown D.C. From there, the tractors filed off the interstate bridge and landed on Fourteenth Street. The farmers then turned onto Independence Avenue toward Twelfth Street and the USDA building, with the first tractors rumbling under the bridge connecting the two sections of the agriculture building complex before daylight.

Madness, pandemonium, anarchy, chaos, road rage, mass confusion— the routes the farmers took were not back roads into D.C. These were the multilane freeways commuters took every day to get into town. Starting out

Four lanes of tractors enter Washington during morning rush hours on February 5, 1979.
Richard Andel.

as a solid line, the tractors were separated into groups of three or four within a current of cars and taxis blowing their horns and giving the farmers hand gestures that they figured out the meanings of very quickly. Tractors went in every direction at once, and some got lost. The rally point was the USDA building, with the lead tractors heading straight toward it. The plan was to completely encircle the complex with tractors and not let anybody in or out, especially Secretary Bergland. But he wasn't going in the building that day anyway, because he had a meeting in Houston, Texas, that morning.

A number of tractors got separated when cars cut into the lines. A tractor going twenty miles per hour wouldn't make much difference to the flow of traffic inside the Beltway, but 3,500 of them, with a truck and a camper behind each one, sure did. Rush hour traffic turned into a parking lot. Lawmakers, lobbyists and office staff got held up for hours that morning and blamed the farmers for every bit of it. From the moment the tractors crossed the river, they disrupted the flow of business in town. The cheering crowds on the overpasses disappeared at the Potomac and were replaced by busy, irritated city folk who didn't want farmers messing up their daily lives. The residents must not have been watching the news stories about the tractorcades coming toward them (like people on the coast not watching the weather during hurricane season). But the D.C. Metro cops were watching, along with the FBI, U.S. Marshal Service, CIA, U.S. Capitol Police, Secret Service, U.S. Park Police and something called the D.C. Protective Services Division.

Every policeman in every jurisdiction and agency was on the clock when the sun came up Monday morning. They attempted to direct the tractors to toward their destination but failed to realize they were dealing with tractors instead of cars. Farmers at the head of the line knew where they were going, which wasn't always the route the police wanted them to take. Most of the lead tractors had a bulldozer blade mounted on the front and a nut behind the wheel. One of the lead farmers put his tractor in park long enough to ask the policemen to move their vehicles out of the way. When the policemen didn't comply, the farmer made a hole with his eight-foot-wide blade. The picture of his John Deere pushing a pile of police motorcycles was printed in several newspapers throughout the country that week. Some of the tractors without blades found it easier to just drive straight over vehicles that had stopped in their way.

Tractors approach Capitol Hill on February 5, 1979. *Richard Andel.*

A farmer from South Georgia drove his Farmall 1256 into town that morning. He drifted along until the column he was in stalled in a thick traffic jam in front of the USDA building. Similar to the farmers who stopped traffic in the middle of Plains the previous Christmas, this farmer put his tractor in park, got down off the seat and busted the fuel bowl. The farmers in line had something special planned to disrupt things. Instead of just walking away with the ignition key, hay bales were shoved under the frames of the tractors, where they would soak up the diesel spurting out—they then set the tractors on fire. The tractors burned, and no vehicle traffic moved down the street until the fires burned themselves out.

The tractorcade wound its way to the National Mall, where the planned rally was to be held on the Capitol steps that afternoon. The preapproved plan was to park on the street next to the mall and walk to the Capitol steps. Instead of parking the tractors in parking spaces, the police motioned the tractors to park in the grass on the mall between Third and Seventh Streets. Some of the first farmers stopped and asked if it was OK to drive out there. The police just waved and reassured them it would be fine.

As soon as the last farmer crossed Third Street and walked to the rally at the Capitol, every bus, garbage truck and tow truck in the D.C. motor pool

A dual-wheeled Farmall 1256 from Ty Ty, Georgia, is burned in front of the USDA building in Washington on February 5, 1979. *Terry Sims.*

Opposite, top: The rally on the Capitol steps after the farmers parked their equipment on the National Mall. Soon, they would realize they were trapped. *Richard Andel.*

Opposite, bottom: Bumper to bumper Metro buses parked along the National Mall, trapping the tractorcade inside. *Richard Andel.*

Above: Dump trucks were used to prevent farmers from driving their tractors off the National Mall. *Richard Andel.*

appeared and lined up bumper to bumper to form a wall around the tractors on the mall, completely blocking in every tractor that had made it across the Potomac. In disbelief, the farmers looked around helplessly as they watched a prison go up around their equipment. The farmers protested, but their protests fell on deaf ears. The police had done their homework and trapped 1,350 tractors on the mall.

The tractorcade's original plan was to park in spaces at the mall, and when the rally on the steps was over, it would travel back to the campground to spend the night. How long were they planning on causing a morning traffic jam? Every day until the goal of 90 percent of parity was achieved. After the initial shock wore off, David Senter and Gerald McCathern discussed the situation. It became an ideal situation to be camped that close, where they

Left: This tractor sat inside the door to the USDA building in the early days of the Washington protest. *Richard Andel.*

Opposite: "Bergland the Bull———— Specialist" button. These buttons were made after Bergland's appearance on national television in February 1979. *Author's collection.*

could take a short walk and be inside the Capitol. From the public's view, it appeared the farmers were right where they'd planned to be all along.

When the farmers looked toward the USDA building, they saw a strange and welcome sight. An unidentified Georgia farmer had made his way onto the roof of the building and replaced the American flag with an American Agriculture Movement flag. Pictures from the early days of the protest show an International tractor sitting inside the doorway of the building. The 1486, or similar model, had miniature AAM flags on both sides of a sign attached to its grill. The sign, with red and blue stenciled letters, read, "This tractor sponsored by Lewis Truck & Tractor Perry, GA."

Sonny Stapleton flew to D.C. in 1979. He recalled:

> *I remember going to Washington, where the farmers had their tractors on the mall. And I didn't take a tractor to Washington. But it was a lot of farmers from Texas, Mississippi, Georgia, drove a tractor all the way to Washington, D.C. We were up there; the police, the Capitol police, were wearing big overcoats. They were big men, I remember that, and they all had a billy stick in their hand. And they didn't take no mess offa no farmer. But they put a fence with buses all the way around the mall and kept the tractors on the mall. They didn't let them ride around town.*

The farmers were treated pretty roughly by the D.C. Police Department. Many of the farmers who went to D.C. remembered the crowds they had

when they caused a ruckus. Though the policemen were big folks, the farmers' least favorite memories were of the horses. The police didn't ride horses because they weren't old enough to drive a car. They would wade those animals into the middle of a crowd, and it would disperse almost immediately.

When the protest's first day was over, nineteen farmers had been arrested. Three of the farmers who were arrested for disorderly conduct were from Georgia, including a young farmer named Johnny Colston from Kite. In jail for assaulting a police officer was the farmer who moved the pile of police motorcycles with his tractor, Kenneth Hilton from Nebraska.

On Tuesday, February 6, Robert Bergland appeared on *Good Morning America* to address the tractors parked in front of the Capitol. In a moment of weakness, he commented that some of the farmers had traveled to D.C., "driven by old-fashioned greed." That afternoon, another rally on the Capitol steps was held and featured appearances by Georgia congressman "Bo" Ginn and Maynard Jackson, the mayor of Atlanta. Many times during the D.C. protest in 1979, a quote surfaced from William Jennings Bryan: "If the cities were destroyed, they would be built again. But if the farms were destroyed, grass would grow in the streets of the cities."

The farmers had originally planned on holding tractorcades in town whenever they wanted to. But the police weren't going to allow them to drive all over town and hold up traffic every minute of every day. After a meeting between the two sides, a compromise was reached. The farmers could leave and drive to a location for a protest at 1:00 p.m. every day if they told the police where they were going. Near the entrance of the Metro subway, there was an opening in the wall of buses guarded by the D.C. Metro Police. When the AAM wanted to have a tractorcade, they negotiated with the police and were released to drive to that location to protest. One of the first locations the farmers chose after being boxed in by the buses was a short drive on Wednesday to the USDA building, where Independence Avenue was completely blocked by tractors for several hours.

Thursday, February 8, was a busy day. In the morning, Robert Bergland and Lynn Daft from the president's staff met with farmers Gene Schroder and Gerald McCathern for an hour and a half in what was described as an

VISITOR'S PASS

U.S. House of Representatives

WASHINGTON, D.C. 2 - 6 - 79

for the Ninety-sixth Congress

B- 32727

M.C.

Please see reverse side for Rules of the Gallery

As a guest of your Representative, we trust that your visit to the House Chamber will be pleasant.

Rules of the Gallery are simple:

Nothing may be taken into the Galleries other than articles of clothing and handbags.

Guests are to be seated at all times and refrain from reading, writing, smoking, eating, drinking and applauding.

Leaning on, or over, or placing articles on the front railing is forbidden.

Hats may not be worn by gentlemen except for religious purposes.

This pass will be honored at House Gallery Doors during the entire Ninety-sixth Congress, except on the occasion of Joint Sessions or unless otherwise advised.

This pass is not transferable, and may be used only by the person whose name appears on the front.

Above: A visitor's pass to Capitol Hill in Washington, D.C., signed by U.S. representative Bo Ginn, 1979. *Terry Sims.*

Opposite: Only one opening was provided in the wall of buses holding the farmers on the National Mall near the Metro subway station, and it was guarded by D.C. Police. *Richard Andel.*

amicable discussion, but no progress was made. The meeting helped ease some of the tension that had grown between the two sides after the rough start on Monday. All the goodwill earned at the meeting was lost when other striking farmers requested to have a tractorcade at the American Farm Bureau office, right down the street from the White House on Pennsylvania Avenue. The farmers drove through town, parked in the middle of the street and crammed themselves into the AFBA lobby. Three sides to the story exist about what happened next: the Farm Bureau's, the American Agriculture Movement's and the D.C. Police Department's. The AFBA office staff said the farmers made a mess in the lobby and put out cigarettes in the carpet, while some of them threw pots out the upstairs windows into the street. The farmers said they didn't see anything like that, and the police found nothing to report. When the tractors blocked Pennsylvania Avenue, the police rerouted traffic instead of getting into another standoff. The police who witnessed the farmers entering the building saw nothing being thrown out of the windows. Allan Grant, the president of the AFBA and a popular target of the strikers, was in Chicago at the time of the farmers' visit. As reported by the *Atlanta Journal Constitution*, when asked about the protest, Grant told reporters, "The problems of farmers aren't going to be solved

A view of the Capitol dome from the tractorcade campground across the Lincoln Memorial Reflecting Pool. *Richard Andel.*

by wrecking crews that take the law into their own hands. The problems of agriculture need our best minds and not our worst emotions."

At a rally on the mall that same day, Alvin Jenkins threatened to drive a tractor through the halls of the USDA building. A parade of tractors drove to the front door of the building and stopped. The lead farmer got off his tractor and met eye to eye with a police captain from the D.C. Protective Services Division, as he had been rushed over from his office nearby to prevent any carnage. The farmer repeated Jenkins's threat but pulled out a toy J.I. Case tractor from inside his coat. The captain was relieved that the tractor wasn't full size but impounded it anyway.

15

WASHINGTON GOT MY GOAT—AGAIN!

O n Thursday, February 8, there were still 625 of the original 1,350 tractors, trucks and campers sitting on the National Mall. On Friday, 100 of the remaining tractors requested to leave and were escorted across the district line to trucks that were waiting to take them home. One of the local Georgia farmers loaded up after a week and had to travel into Maryland for brake work on his truck. After paying his bill, he and another farmer shared the driving duties and left Washington. They arrived in Soperton after about ten hours, instead of the ten days it took to get to D.C. When the farmers unloaded the first tractor and parted ways, one farmer said to the other, "I love you like a brother. But I need some time by myself to recover!"

The weather was cold when the tractorcade left home, but it got worse when they arrived in D.C. Sonny Stapleton remembered dealing with the winter weather: "I remember knit britches, trousers, were in style. There was a man laying on one of those vents out there on the sidewalk. The building was heated with steam, and it was coming up through there, so he was sleeping on it. There were two or three of us standing on that vent, because it was warm. I remember that very well, and when I stepped off of it, my britches froze! 'Cause they had gotten wet from that steam, and they froze. You talkin' about a mess!"

The campers on the mall were divided into sections by state. The Georgia section was located near the Capitol Steps Reflecting Pool in front of the Ulysses S. Grant Memorial. The Lincoln Memorial Reflecting Pool could

Georgia tractors sit on the National Mall during the farmer protest in Washington in 1979. *Richard Andel.*

Adam Andel poses in front of his tractor and camper after the snow on the National Mall in 1979. *Richard Andel.*

"I Was a P.O.W. in Carter's Compound Wash., D.C., AAM 1979" button. *Author's collection.*

be found at the west end of the mall. Firewood collecting was not allowed, but it happened. Benches were reportedly torn up, and trees were cut down and burned for heat. After witnesses complained, the farmers were allowed to buy propane to heat their campers.

On Tuesday, February 13, the farmers marched on Capitol Hill with their hands in the air, proclaiming themselves to be "POWs in Carter's compound." They climbed the steps with their hands in the air, telling lawmakers and reporters they were "prisoners of Washington."

The week after the farmers' arrival, the *Washington Post* printed a number of articles and opinion pieces about the strike that the farmers considered false. On Friday, February 16, the farmers had had enough. A tractorcade was organized in the direction of the *Washington Post*, and after a couple of minutes, tractors had the place surrounded. No one could enter the building, and no deliveries could be made in or out. Farmers showed the workers inside their opinion of the paper by burning stacks of it in front of the building. A quick meeting was held between the farmers and the *Washington Post*'s staff, spearheaded by Tommy Fulford. He told the Associated Press, "They agreed they don't know a h— of a lot about agriculture. They know a lot more now."

Reporters have often compared current damage done to the mall to the damage that was caused when the tractorcade was in town. There was at least one tractor burned on the mall every day, including an old John Deere cotton picker that was hauled in from Texas with "Politician Eater" painted on it. Using diesel fuel, farmers burned "AAM" into the grass at the foot of the Capitol steps, knowing every politician could see it if they looked that way. There was a Georgia farmer on a Farmall tractor who was seen in the Reflection Pool in all the newspapers, busting up a thick layer of ice that had formed. One of the farmers I interviewed told me about driving his tractor on the steps of the Lincoln Memorial and lamented that kind of thing would never happen again.

The politicians, office staff, city workers and news media didn't want these new campers in town. Reporters did their best to portray the farmers as a menacing group of vigilantes seeking to destroy the Capitol. An American

Farm Bureau spokesman told the media that they had been tracking public support for farmers since 1973. The percentage of people who viewed farmers in a negative light was normally 8 to 9 percent. But the recent protests had caused that number to skyrocket, all the way up to 11 percent. When asked if the president's lack of support from farmers would affect him in the long run, Robert Bergland speculated that Jimmy Carter would be reelected in 1980.

On Sunday, February 18, while Donnie Allison and Cale Yarborough fought in the grass after crashing during the last lap of the first nationally televised Daytona 500, a winter storm blew into D.C. and dropped twenty-six inches of snow. Vehicles couldn't move. Doctors couldn't make it to the hospitals, because ice and snow made the streets impassable. The farmers and their tractors were called on to clear the roads and dig out buried police cars. One farmer traveled to fetch a newspaper reporter who was stranded at home only days after the farmers had surrounded his office for releasing a tirade criticizing the farmers in their protest efforts. As the reporter rode in the cab for a much shorter distance than the farmer drove to get to D.C., he realized the amount of effort it took for the farmer to drive 1,500 miles to be there. Folks all over town were singing the farmers' praises. But when the snow melted after a couple of days, everybody went back to their antagonistic ways.

There were spies among the crowd of farmers who tried to infiltrate the group. High-spirited, low-knowledge individuals stuck out like sore thumbs when they tried to dress and talk like farmers. Then their plans changed. The spies began to jog through the lines of tractors, collecting intel. Some of the spies tried to blend in using cross country skis through the area. Nobody knew where the spies had come from or what they were looking for, but Gerald Long could pick out a spy from a mile away. Once, a couple of spies, a middle-aged man and woman, came jogging through the camp together. When they came too close to the entrance door on one of the campers, the door opened and *swat*! The man broke his glasses and fell to the ground. As he gathered himself back up, he and the woman ran out of the mall as fast as they could, and they weren't seen again.

On Friday, February 23, the last bit of mischief was committed in front of the White House. A final tractorcade was requested with the destination of 1600 Pennsylvania Avenue. The remaining tractors lined up, with one farmer concealing an old hairy goat inside a piece of equipment. The farmers disobeyed the policemen's request to keep moving and blocked all the lanes in the street directly in front of the White House. Several arrests

Top: The Capitol dome from the AAM campground on the National Mall after the snow in February 1979. *Jerome and Teresa Wells.*

Bottom: The Georgia territory of the campground on the National Mall. *Richard Andel.*

were made, including that of a young man who was charged with throwing a thresher over the White House fence. The goat was not inside that machine but landed on the lawn afterward. The goat had been kept on the mall inside an antique, stationary grain threshing machine with a sign on it that read, "This is Carter's Farm Program Computer. Otis, Colorado."

When the tractors returned to the mall, police sent word that they were not going to allow another tractorcade in D.C., and it was time to bring the protest to an end. The AAM that was proud to say it was leaderless had to nominate a farmer to negotiate its withdrawal. Tommy Kersey from Unadilla was chosen to hammer out the details. No progress was made by either side for

Opposite, top: The antique thresher where the White House goat was kept. It was parked on the National Mall with the goat inside. *Richard Andel.*

Opposite, bottom: The White House right after the goat was released on the lawn. *Richard Andel.*

Above: The final protest at the Federal Reserve prior to the dispersal of the tractorcade in March 1979. *Richard Andel.*

almost a week before the police requested a committee to negotiate instead. The police offered the chance for one more tractorcade anywhere in the district the farmers chose in exchange for a dramatic reduction in the number of tractors on the mall. The farmers agreed and chose the Federal Reserve as their last destination, and they included a request for several farmers to meet with the Federal Reserve chairman G. William Miller and any of the other members of the board. Representing AAM in its last "official" D.C. meeting were Bud Bittner, Gerald McCathern, Tommy Kersey and Tommy Fulford. Every tractor and farmer that remained made the trip. No tangible results from the March 1 meeting have ever been recorded.

After the Federal Reserve meeting, the farmers were given short notice to move their tractors from the mall and onto the side streets. Tractors that were not moved in a timely manner were pulled off the mall and into parking spaces, making some of the worst ruts and damage seen on the mall during the entire event. All but 50 machines had until Sunday, March 4, to leave. When the Andels left D.C. to go home that day, there were still 283 tractors on the mall. The 50 tractors parked on the street near the mall and 2 parked at the USDA building were symbols of defiance against the USDA and the president. Several tractors were still impounded after their operators were unable to prove ownership.

After the farmers left Washington, Marvin Trice recalled, "We might have quit too quick up there in Washington. We were probably getting on their nerves being in them offices all the time. 'Cause I went up'there two different weeks, two different times, maybe three. We visited all them offices up there—senators and congressmen. I think we probably got ol' Herman Talmadge out of there, because he didn't get reelected."

In politics, money talks and matters. It would seem the only thing people in Washington wanted to think about was how much the tractorcade was going to cost the city. The damage to the National Mall was estimated to cost $500,000. Adding in overtime salaries for D.C. and Park Service Police pushed the estimate over $2.5 million. The USDA secretary and Park Service listed items damaged, including seven trees and ten park benches that had been destroyed. When they attempted to pad the expense report, their hand was called. Two damaged light poles were blamed on the tractors. After further review, one pole had damage 30 feet off the ground, and the other was seen on the ground by an AAM member who was scouting the area the day before the tractors' arrival. How 6,500 cubic feet of dirt was missing from the mall is anybody's guess. On the day the agriculture secretary tried to pin damage from a farmer driving through the Reflection Pool, there was a Park Service tractor that was bigger than the Farmall that was seen in the newspapers driving through the icy water and a loaded dump truck observed parked inside the drained Reflection Pool.

When the last tractors left the mall, Gerald McCathern and a group of Maryland farmers volunteered their time and equipment to repair the field. Using the same International Harvester 1486 he used to bring the tractorcade to Washington, he plowed the ground. The farmers all donated grass seed and covered the bare earth. Although the mall was in bad shape in 1979, the same farmers who protested there repaired it, and numerous people have told me that the mall never looked better than it did after the farmers repaired it.

The farmers' protest didn't have long to linger. At 4:00 a.m. on Wednesday, March 28, 1979, a major nuclear incident at Three Mile Island

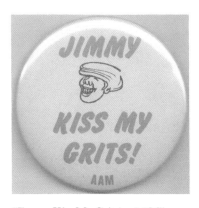

"Jimmy, Kiss My Grits!—AAM" button. *Author's collection.*

in Pennsylvania's Susquehanna River stole all the attention of the public, the media, and the president. Although plenty of activities and protests were led by the American Agriculture Movement over the next few years, the tractorcade and its fifteen minutes of fame were history.

Prior to the Washington protest, the farmers were proud to be a "leaderless lot." When they left town, they realized that was a bad thing. Some things were accomplished but nothing like what some of them who had driven two thousand miles expected. At a meeting following the protest, the AAM directed Tommy Kersey to lead an exploratory committee into the possibility of the organization forming a lobbying office. They realized the Washington crowd had professional lobbyists in on the long game, not hobby lobbyists who showed up unannounced and expected results for nothing—by nothing, that meant no cash paid out.

One morning, Tommy Kersey awoke to a surprise: he was running for vice president of the United States. He was just as surprised as anyone else, because an organization other than the American Agriculture Movement had nominated him. The group was called the Ownership Group, which nominated candidates for president and vice president, for both the Democrat and Republican tickets. Kersey's nomination didn't appear on any ballots on Super Tuesday, though.

During the month of April, Paul Harvey produced a column comparing wheat to another commodity that had skyrocketed in the last few years:

FARMERS TO THE RESCUE

If we need oil and the oil countries need grain, why don't we swap? Historically, in effect, we did. But then in 1973, the oil nations decided to multiply their asking price for oil. But we did not increase our asking price for food grains. It's not too late. Until the OPEC nations got their heads together and decided to blackmail us for ever-higher oil prices, the price of a bushel of wheat and a barrel of crude was about the same: $2. On the *world exchanges, the two commodities had been neck and neck for years: $2 wheat, $2 oil. Now, in 1979, foreign oil producers have escalated crude oil prices to more than $14 a barrel. But wheat is still selling for $2 or $3 a bushel. Make no mistake, the United States controls or has the autonomy to control the world price for wheat and other food grains. We represent 40 to 50 percent of the total world market in this commodity. Japan and the European Economic Community (EEC) countries are the major importers of American grain, and it is in those countries that our dollar is in the most trouble. Japan purchases American wheat for $2.50 to $3 a bushel, then adds a tariff when it reaches her shores to increase the price to Japanese millers to more than $9 a bushel. A $6-a-bushel tariff is a windfall for that government. Is it not we who should be getting that markup? Better still, why not peg the price of wheat to the price of oil, then, even if the OPEC nations should elect to charge us $100 a barrel it would balance out. More logically, however, the result would be to hold the prices of both commodities down, as the law of supply and demand did hold them down for decades preceding 1973.*

One out of three harvested acres in the United States goes for export. Because our farmers have been so efficient, we have been much too generous with our neighbors. Any objective evaluation of world oil consumption and production projected a few decades down the road confirms that the oil rich nations of the Middle East will exhaust their reserves. If history repeats itself, and it usually does, those now-fat nations will look to us again for handouts in the lean years. Perhaps we should encourage them to emulate the biblical Joseph, who wisely set aside grain in preparation for a time of famine. And if they are not wise enough to do so on their own, we should encourage them to put their money in food rather than in lavish living. We could rebalance our foreign trade and strengthen our dollar abroad and at home by serving notice now: a bushel of wheat for a barrel of oil. Take it or leave it.

Currently, oil is averaging around one hundred dollars a barrel, while wheat is about eight dollars a bushel.

Paul Harvey then examined the farmer's situation in late 1979:

The next world battlefield will be the farm. It is entirely possible and increasingly likely that food-producing nations will close ranks as oil-producing nations already have. And any American policymaker who can't see this opportunity is wearing blinders! It could happen as soon as 10 years from now. Any grotesque inequity eventually is its own undoing. U.S. farmers have been getting the short end of the stick for generations. They have failed to participate in the prosperity which they have created for the rest of us. Heretofore, they have put up with it because the freewheeling, individualistic nature of the farmer resisted regimentation, even in his own interest. That is changing. From 1952 to 1977, prices paid to farmers increased 6%. During those same years, the cost of farming increased 122%! But they suffered the squeeze because they had no viable alternative. Now they have. The so-called family farm is being phased out in favor of the factory farm. Some of us might not prefer it that way. But that's the way it is. Family farms have decreased from 6.8 million in the thirties to only 2.7 million today. That number will be down to one million in just five more years. So—and this is significant—already 70% of all American farmland is owned by 15% of the landowners. Five more years, and 75% of all food production in the United States will be under direct corporate control. Granted, big government could prevent a corporate monopoly, even as it has prevented corporate industrial monopolies, but should it? The rest of the world caught up with us in industrial production. Over the horizon, overpopulated nations may learn to harvest the oceans, but there's nothing like that in the foreseeable future. As is, and for as far ahead as anybody can see, the United States, Canada, Argentina and Australia produce and can control 80% of the world's food grain supply. Our arable soil will not last forever; fertility depletes as surely as oil reserves do. We have altogether as much right as the oil-exporting nations to demand a fairer price for our major cash crop. We have no more moral obligation to feed the world than they have to fuel the world. Further, exhausting our fertility in an effort to feed others diminishes their incentive to feed themselves. The next war will be between the stork and the plow. The battlefield will be the farm.

16

JOHNNY COLSTON

The struggle during the farm strike years hit farmers of all sizes, not just the big ones. There were folks from outside the hotbeds in Dooly and Bacon Counties. A name that came up frequently with an amazing story to tell was Johnny Colston from Kite. I called folks I knew from Kite; some told me that he was dead, while others said he was still alive. They couldn't all be right, so I headed there to see if I could find him—or at least his grave.

A few days before Easter, a tornado came through the middle of Kite and knocked out power to several homes. It even toppled some of the headstones in a cemetery over there. I went into town and saw the damage from the storm that cut straight across Highway 221 like a giant weed eater. At the Dollar General, I asked the manager if she knew Johnny Colston. She said she did and pointed me toward his farm. At the corner of two dirt roads, I found a store draped with Trump 2024 flags and a farmhouse that the recent tornado had missed by about thirty yards. An older man was cleaning up the yard with a chainsaw and a UTV. I got out of my truck and still didn't know what I was going to do.

"How you doin'?"

"I'm alright. We just had a little wind. Missed the house by a little bit. Got that big oak right there. That chainsaw's done whipped me today!"

"I'm looking for a man that drove a tractor from here to Washington in 1979. He got there, and they put one of his eyes out. Named Johnny Colston."

He turned and looked straight at me, where I could see his left eye was completely missing.

"That'd be me. They shot this eye out with a riot gun, point blank."

Getting a farmer to recall events from the late '70s can be like cranking an old car that has been under a shelter since that time. I knew there hadn't been a major news story about Mr. Colston since the early '80s, so I wasn't sure how much he could remember. We visited for a few minutes and talked, and after he felt like he had his thoughts together about February 5, 1979, we sat on the porch of his store as he told a story that couldn't have been more incredible from beginning to end.

I don't know if you remember it, but in 1977, it was a heck of a drought. I wasn't never a big farmer, but I had about 350 acres of corn that year. I never pulled one ear. It got that blight in it. Even the nubbins, you couldn't even let the cows eat it. That's what set it off. We were just in terrible shape after that year and started protesting. But the congressmen and senators, they didn't want to do nothing to help them. They went to Plains down there in '77, where Carter was from, trying to get him to help. Then in '78, they went to Washington, D.C., in buses; they didn't drive their tractors.

Then they set up a big tractorcade in '79—the line we went in on. There were tractors all the way from Washington state; they had left home a couple of weeks before we even had to leave. But we all joined up to hit I-95 and went straight up on up into Washington. We had the state patrol ahead of us. At night, sitting side of the road, we'd camp. Some of them would have a little camper pulling behind their tractor. They'd sleep in it. And it was cold 'cause it was like in January.

Colston started out from Kite, driving a brand-new Massey-Ferguson 1135 with a cab that had been donated for him to drive to Washington by the local Massey-Ferguson dealer. The tractor had a sign on the front that read, "Washington or Bust Johnson County, Georgia." After meeting up with other area farmers, he took off toward I-75 to head north toward Washington. One of the farmers in line suggested to the Georgia State Patrol that they should have the tractors travel in the left-hand lane on the interstate instead of the right to make it easier for cars to get on and off. Although it seemed like a good idea, the suggestion was not used.

There has always been plenty of speculation about how that many tractors could go that far without filling up on diesel. "We never bought diesel fuel. Fuel distributors, everywhere we were, came out where we were and fueled us up for free every night when we'd park to camp. We drove them tractors to get their attention, figuring they'd do something if they see all these tractors coming into Washington."

What happened when we got to town the first morning, that was the darndest traffic jam you ever did see. The policemen were trying to direct them. But we started going in there at about the same time them people started going to work up there in Washington. Everything was just on lockdown! Them policemen were trying to get those tractors to move and get the cars to move. They directed us; I was in a line of traffic headed up a street where there was nothing but cars. A policeman pulled up and told us to get on the sidewalk and go on past those cars. Well, we started going up past them cars until we went as far as we could go till we came to another roadblock, and there we was on the sidewalk.

Somebody on an International tractor, which is red, had run over the hood of a car somewhere, and the policemen were looking for the tractor. I was on a Massey-Ferguson, and they saw that red tractor and they thought it was me! I was sitting still in the line, and they came and knocked the glass out of the tractor. They shot me in the face with a shotgun loaded with riot control chemical and put my eye out because they thought I was the other tractor. Later on, they found out I wasn't, and I sued their butt. Anyway, it was too late. My eye was gone. But still, we got no help from the government, except for lip service. You know what I'm talking about? And I'm about ready to go back up there again! I still got one eye!

Earlier on the morning of February 5, the striking farmers formed a circle of tractors around the USDA building. At the intersection of Independence Avenue and Seventh Street, Johnny Colston was sitting in line for what other farmers said was about five minutes before police beat the glass door out of his tractor and threw a tear gas canister filled with CS gas into the cab to run him out. The police pulled Colston out; one slung him over his shoulders and hauled him off to jail with eighteen other farmers. It's unimaginable, but he was not identified or located by the other farmers in his group for several hours as he laid in the jail, covered in tear gas with permanent eye damage and burning lungs. When another local farmer found him, his lawyer demanded the jail staff get Colston to a hospital and have him released. In the ambulance and at the hospital, five nurses and policemen were overcome by the fumes on Johnny Colston's clothes. The medical staff removed and burned his clothes, and when they got him patched up, the police came and tried to put him back in jail. Instead, he went to the Washington Mall with the other striking farmers and stayed for about a week. The Massey-Ferguson dealer in Tennille sent a trailer to Washington to retrieve the tractor. They replaced the shattered glass but had to leave it open for a couple of months to let the fumes from the tear gas die down.

Johnny Colston made his way back to Kite after losing his left eye and winning an excessive use of force case against the D.C. Police. He served as chief deputy for many years with the Johnson County Sheriff's Department. Then he was elected Johnson County magistrate judge in the early 1990s. He farmed and raised catfish for several years. When the economy tanked back in 2007 and 2008, he and his wife moved to North Dakota, where he ran a bulldozer for a couple of years on a project installing electricity generating windmills.

Several farmers from Kite went to Washington, including an older farmer named Hines Martin. The group had a meeting with USDA undersecretary John White during the Washington trip in which they discussed cotton. Hines Martin had been growing cotton since he was old enough to hold the plow handles straight behind his father's mule. The undersecretary asked if they needed any assistance with their crop. The answer was yes. Mister White said, "We've got a pamphlet around here somewhere that might can help you." That's as good an example of the disconnection between the farmers and Washington.

Let me tell you this. It was kinda funny. They got us all on what they call the mall. It's a seventy-five-acre street between the Washington Monument and the Capitol up there. And they blocked us in with these big transit buses. They blocked the exits. So, there we were, camping out on the mall for a week, you know? After about the fourth day, them guys would get on them tractors. Them guys weren't good fellas like me! They's mean, and they had a blade on the tractor, and they'd push up bushes and stuff out there, them shrubs. One guy drove his tractor up the Capitol steps, a big ol' four-wheel-drive tractor. A couple of them accidentally run into the Reflection Pond at night. But about the fourth day, the policemen come out there and said, "Let me ask you a question. We hadn't seen y'all come out of there to get no fuel for them tractors and they're steady running. Y'all must have brought a lot of fuel with you." We said, "No! Them buses is full of it right there!" We were going out at night and getting the fuel out of the buses and running the tractors all day. Then at night, we'd go get some more out. It was a fun trip, even though it turned out like it did. We got to meet a lot of people in the same business.

17

EVICTION

With high interest rates, low commodity prices and higher input costs for a period of over five years, the government's solution of loans instead of price supports turned farmers' financial situations sour. When banks and financial institutions ran out of patience in the early '80s, FmHA, the Production Credit Association and the Federal Land Bank started making foreclosures at breakneck speed. By 1983, FmHA held nearly five times the number of farms in foreclosure than it had two years earlier. With emotions running high, the roller coaster ride started and didn't slow down until desperate measures were taken.

The pinch of recession was being felt in the agricultural equipment manufacturing industry in the early 1980s. In 1981, Allis-Chalmers reported an 82 percent profit loss as the first sign of trouble. Then two worker strikes crippled Caterpillar and International Harvester. After the International Harvester strike ended, the company took an eighteen-month loss, totaling over $1 billion, and sought to restructure nearly $4 billion in corporate debt. The restructuring was approved and proclaimed as an American success story, but the recovery was short-lived. Tenneco consumed International Harvester and merged the company's line with J.I. Case. Even John Deere's sales showed consecutive losses for the same period. But their losses of $28 million and $11 million were one-tenth the size of International Harvester's losses.

Auction companies began having their services requested throughout farming country and didn't expect to operate under the threat of violence and disorder, especially from people they knew or with whom they shared a last name. When an individual, such as a farmer, needed to borrow money, they used a bank or lending service, with the deed to a piece of property, ownership of farm equipment or even livestock handed over to the lender as collateral. The borrower had pay on their loan's balance within a specified period agreed upon at the time of the issuance of the loan by all parties involved. If there were circumstances that prevented timely repayment, an extension could be issued by the lender. If no money was collected within the timeframe with no extension given, the farm would come under foreclosure. Notices were issued by the lender and carried out by the sheriff's department. Legal notices appeared in the local newspaper for four weeks to remove the element of surprise. If the loan was not paid off, the farm was sold on the courthouse steps on the first Tuesday of the month.

Sometimes, different banks or creditors had liens against different properties on a single farm and didn't work well together to help farmers stay afloat in the 1980s. One out-of-state dairy farmer had his cattle repossessed first. The creditor liquidated the herd by sending them to the abattoir and got ground beef out of them instead of milk. Another creditor repossessed the farm equipment next, making it impossible for the farmer to produce anything on the land. Finally, the land was auctioned off by another creditor, because the farmer couldn't make his payments.

Farmland put up as collateral would usually start with a small piece of land with little or no sentimental value. After several bad farming years were strung together in the 1970s and 1980s, homesteads were transferred from families that had lived there for generations to banks and insurance companies located over one thousand miles away. When the new owner was ready to liquidate the property, an eviction notice was delivered by a constable or other representative from the sheriff's office. Banks and insurance companies were poor landlords and weren't aspiring farmers. When the time came to sell, there was an established reserve price equal to the amount owed by the previous owner, but it was not the resale value of the property. If the reserve price wasn't met, the seller reserved the right to refuse the sale.

Many meetings and plans were made between the first missed loan payment and the appearance of farmers' names in the legal notices. Social disorder didn't occur until the eviction notices were delivered. A farm could be sold on paper easily enough, but the actual removal of a family from their home was never amicable and sometimes became violent. Preventing the completion of a farm sale would not negate the loan balance owed. That small detail didn't stop a whole host of farmers throughout the country from trying.

As the farm evictions of the early 1980s marched on, the American Agriculture Movement experienced a paralyzing split between the two groups that started it all: the unorganized grassroots effort and the national organization. The fracturing split appeared at the 1982 national meeting in Minot, North Dakota. At the meeting, the organization voted to stop communicating with its own newspaper, the *American Agriculture News*, which ceased operations in December 1983. Since the national organization charged yearly dues, the power of each state to create bylaws and elect national officers depended solely on how much money that state had sent to the organization. One paying member even suggested that people shouldn't be allowed to wear AAM caps if they hadn't paid their dues.

On January 4, 1983, one of the founding fathers of the American Agriculture Movement, Jerry Wright, lost his farm to foreclosure. He stood and watched as the Federal Land Bank conducted the sale on the Baca County Courthouse steps. Several hundred farmers, all wearing red bananas on their left arms, attempted to stop the sale. The farmers tried to shout down the auctioneer, but the 320-acre farm was sold back to FLB for what was owed: $92,000. After the gavel fell, several farmers tried to continue the sale as the auctioneer and sheriff's deputies retreated inside the building. The crowd at the door was maced after three farmers made it inside. As the crowd refused to leave, tear gas was dropped out of a window above. Handcuffed, one of the detained farmers broke free by jumping out a window. The whole thing was televised locally. The images of farmers protesting, being gassed and appearing bloodied to TV was too much to ignore. ABC took three of the AAM leaders in a private jet to appear on *Nightline* that evening. Jerry Wright appeared on the *Today Show* the next morning.

The next national meeting was held in January in Nashville, where the final chapter played out. At the front door, armed guards were posted at check-in to enforce a twenty-five-dollar entry fee. Inside the convention, two events dominated the conversation: Jerry Wright's foreclosure and what was known as the Great Soybean Raid, which was still playing out in Missouri. Opinions about how to handle the two situations varied between two groups with different ideologies. One group believed in letting the courts sort it out, while the other believed in taking the law into their own hands. Two men emerged as symbols of the two ideologies dividing the farmers. AAM Inc. felt it was necessary to have a permanent lobbying office in Washington, D.C., while the grassroots folks thought the idea was sacrilegious. The man in charge of the lobbying office in Washington was David Senter from Texas. One of the founding fathers from Colorado, Alvin Jenkins, had been selected as the national grassroots spokesman and was expected to run for national president. Jenkins's group believed that protests and tractorcades were the most effective methods to cause a change. The members' vote was split and elected Tennessee's state president Tommy Willis as national president. He spoke to the group and vowed to support all AAM efforts. Everyone went home believing a collapse had been avoided. But as soon as everyone got home, the AAM organization began to wilt back to the area where it was first organized, where it is still in existence today.

Foreclosures in 1983 and 1984 were delayed thanks to a class-action lawsuit against the FmHA's foreclosure of a Screven County farm owned by Inez and Remer Curry in 1979. That case, which held conflicting rulings from courts in Georgia and Alabama, helped spawn suits against the FmHA in forty-seven states. The case sought to prove the FmHA had wrongly pursued foreclosure on the Currys by not informing them of a debt deferral option that was available. The FmHA did not attempt to foreclose on the farm to cause them to default in the '70s. It just chose not to lend the Currys any money to farm for several years, causing their operation to grind to a halt. While the court case crept along, the Currys were forced into retirement. The FmHA's Georgia state director believed the case was preventing the natural process of farmers going out of business and having their farms closed out. In August 1984, the Georgia Eleventh Circuit Court of Appeals said the FmHA had not enacted the deferral program outlined by the law. The USDA, which oversaw the program, could appeal to the Supreme Court but chose not to. About a month later, President Reagan released a four-point relief plan to ease the FmHA debt burden held by farmers, including up to five years' worth of deferral, or $100,000 in interest or principal. At the time, the FmHA held loans of $1.2 billion on 9,200 Georgia farmers, and well over half were behind on their payments. Two months later, the only state to vote for Walter Mondale and Geraldine Ferraro in the presidential election was Mondale's home state of Minnesota.

In 1984, two movies were released about the plight of American farms: *The River*, starring Mel Gibson and Sissy Spacek; and *Country*, starring Sam Shepard and Jessica Lange. Musicians from different genres recorded songs to focus attention on the problem, including Merle Haggard, John Cougar Mellencamp and the Charlie Daniels Band. In 1985, Merle Haggard organized a train tour through the country in support of the American farmer, while Willie Nelson met with other musicians and farmers in Illinois to plan what became known as Farm Aid. One of the original organizers and founders of Farm Aid was David Senter from the American Agriculture Movement. The first Farm Aid was held at the University of Illinois, with performances from Nelson, Bob Dylan, Waylon Jennings, B.B. King and the Beach Boys. The concert was sold out in less than two days, with ticket prices at $17.50.

After a short pause, farm auctions and protesters resumed their battle in Sylvester in February 1985 at the Worth County Courthouse. The sale of a 588-acre farm was the result of a disaster program loan of $96,000 that was issued in 1977 by the Small Business Administration (SBA). Since the SBA had not received any payments in six years, the debt had swollen to over $100,000. When the auctioneer attempted to begin the sale, the protesters, including Tommy Kersey, began singing their song to the melody of "Home on the Range."

> *Oh, give me my farm,*
> *And the price that is fair,*
> *And a chance to pay all my debts.*
> *I'll work hard and long,*
> *On my farm I belong,*
> *I beg you not to take it yet.*

When the SBA officials attempted to start the bidding, the crowd sang the song again. After several more tries, the attempts to make the sale were stopped. The SBA officials went inside the courthouse and decided to delay the sale for a couple of months. Shortly after stopping the auction, Kersey met with State Representatives Larry Walker from Perry and Paul Trulock from Climax to discuss a moratorium on farm foreclosures. The information discussed was relayed to Joe Frank Harris, the governor. He wrote a letter to Congress in Washington, urging the moratorium.

Less than two weeks later, a foreclosure sale was scheduled for a 674-acre farm between Milan and McRae. Ralph Foster, a local agribusinessman, had fallen on hard times like everyone else in the industry. His farm supply store dried up when his customers couldn't buy new equipment or pay what they owed on their old stuff. The Foster Brothers Farm was advertised as "One of the Best Farms in Telfair County" and included several houses, a pecan orchard with a storage warehouse, hay fields and some of the most picturesque fishing ponds imaginable. Early Saturday morning, onlookers and protesters began arriving from both ends of Red Hill Road. The Roy Holland Auctioneering Company got the pleasure of attempting to sell the property for the Mutual of New York Insurance Company after holding the property for nearly a year.

The gavel hit to begin the auction as a rousing chorus of the same unnamed song from the Worth County sale began to drown out the auctioneer. After a few more attempts that only got a louder response as more people joined in after they learned all the words, Roy Holland met with Tommy Kersey, the insurance company and Ralph Foster's son Frank. The insurance company agreed to postpone the sale of the farm and lease the place to Frank until the end of the year, with an option to purchase it back at that time. The biggest loser that day was Roy Holland, to the tune of about $15,000, for surveying, advertising, paying his bid catchers, et cetera. When the year was over, the Foster family's time was up, and it was time to pack up or pay up. At Christmas, the farm was bought by Ralph's longtime neighbor and sometimes competitor, with the houses sold back to the family.

A week and a half after the attempted auction in Telfair County, the circus moved to the Baker County Courthouse in the middle of Newton. A newly formed organization called the National Farm Products Minimum Pricing Union showed up to protest and was headed by none other than Tommy Kersey. The proceedings were overseen by Sheriff Hopson Irvin and a lawyer from Camilla named James C. Brim. The protesters stole Brim's legal papers a couple of times and played keep-away with him. After the sheriff got the papers back, Brim clutched them under his arm tightly and had to extinguish them a couple of times after somebody set fire to them. The sheriff called for reinforcements from Camilla and the Georgia State Patrol to keep the situation under control. Somehow the sale of two farms totally over 650 acres was completed, despite the crowd's most passionate attempts to stop them.

In July 1985, the protesters attempted to stop the sale of two farmers' properties in Tift County but failed. The farms were good examples of how much money could be owed to several institutions for the same property at the same time. The first farm comprised 408 acres and was sold for $280,000, which was enough to pay back what was owed to the Farm Credit Banks of Columbia. But FmHA took possession of the tract because the farmer still owed $408,000. The other tract comprised 50 acres and was sold for $30,000, the amount owed to the SBA. FmHA took possession of the second tract because it was owed $199,000 on the property.

The auction companies and banks fought their way through and dropped the gavel more times than not for the rest of the summer and into the fall. Everything was rolling along smoothly until a bank in Cochran foreclosed on a man named Oscar Lorick.

18

SOMETHING BREWING
IN BLECKLEY COUNTY

T o fill the void left by the American Agriculture Movement, a new organization was formed in Middle Georgia by several farmers facing foreclosure called the National Farm Products Minimum Pricing Union. The group's initial mission was to buy grain and not sell it until a minimum, or floor, price was offered for it. The central office in Unadilla was located inside the original state AAM headquarters and operated by Tommy Kersey.

Farmers were running out of tricks and stall tactics when Kersey made contact with Larry Humphreys in Velma, Oklahoma. Humphreys was a wealthy man with an inheritance he received from his father, who was a banker. Some of his inheritance money was used to organize the Heritage Library and to tour the farming areas of the country, speaking out against the federal government, especially the Federal Reserve. Kersey invited Humphreys to come to Georgia to speak at several NFPMPU meetings. In early November 1985, a pair of meetings were held in Metter and Hawkinsville, with the impending eviction of a Black farmer in Bleckley County the focus of the meetings.

The Lorick farm had been in the family since 1866, originally containing around two thousand acres of farmland near the Ocmulgee River on the Bleckley-Pulaski County line. The land was originally purchased for Amos Lorick at the beginning of the Reconstruction era. He was born in South Carolina before the Civil War and moved to Hawkinsville after the war was over, when his father purchased the land for him to farm. During

Reconstruction, nobody around the Pine Barrens had any money, especially not enough to buy that amount of land. Amos Lorick did very well as a farmer but lost two wives while trying to raise a family. When he was in his seventies, his third wife gave birth to a boy and a girl. His youngest son, named Oscar, was only five years old when Amos died.

Oscar Lorick grew up and tended the farmland of his father, gaining great success raising hogs and producing more peanuts per acre than anyone else in the county. But by the 1980s, the farm had been whittled down to less than eighty acres. Mr. Lorick found himself in financial trouble, like almost every other farmer in those days, and in February 1985, a foreclosure notice for the farm appeared in the *Cochran Journal*. On the first Tuesday of November, a deputy hand delivered a notice from the bank that gave the family until November 15 to leave the property. As word of their situation got out, Tommy Kersey was contacted, and he offered his assistance to the Loricks.

The sheriff of Bleckley County was Ed Coley, a man in his mid-thirties with a department that had four deputies and a secretary. He recalled the story:

> *Oscar Lorick's farm had a lien put on it. Then, in the court, they lost and I was to repossess it. He got into debt and they had a judgment against him. The paperwork got to me to serve on him and he was gonna have to leave.*
>
> *I was warned ahead of time what was about to happen on Oscar's farm. We were having a sheriff's convention in Savannah. I got a call that something was brewing, and they thought I needed to be there. I left Savannah and came to Cochran. I can't tell you exact what I was told, but it hit me enough that I left the convention and came to Cochran that night. My first meeting was with a farmer from Pulaski County. He told me that they had met at some farm in Hawkinsville. They had held meetings like two or three times, and they were fixing to move into Oscar's. This farmer told me, "You need to know." He was trying to tell me how dangerous they were. They were gonna do away with the sheriff's department, GBI, whoever came out. It was gonna be an armed resistance. They were gonna do whatever they had to do. That's why I said, "Man, this ain't gonna happen in Bleckley County. No."*

During the early 1980s, thousands of farms were foreclosed on with some resistance. There were a few high-profile cases in which farmers turned to violence and claimed the lives of law enforcement officers. But that was in the Midwest—not Georgia. The location of this standoff appeared suitable to the armed group due to the small size of the local sheriff's department.

The sheriff continued:

> *I guess because of what I was being told, about how radical they were, that they were gonna prevent us from serving the papers and taking control of the farm for the bank. They were gonna stop it and this part of the country and in this day and time—they were farfetched. At that point, I still didn't believe it. Anyway, I came in and was trying to, from the information I had, to decipher what was gonna be, what I was gonna do, what I wasn't gonna do to respond. My whole thing was, let's not respond and let's see what they're gonna do. I didn't want them to do anything that would give it a headline and do nothing that would put anybody in jeopardy.*
>
> *But that farmer in Pulaski County, he really helped me. He gave me time, if it was true. Because at that time, I didn't doubt the farmer. But you just don't believe something like that is gonna happen in Bleckley County. He gave me time so I could put everything on my plate so it wouldn't just hit me in the face and me or a deputy or some neighbor might overreact.*

The farmer who met with the sheriff had been to a meeting of the NFPMPU led by Tommy Kersey and Larry Humphreys. The plan at the meeting was reportedly to have an armed standoff with the government and cause a "Kent State–style" confrontation. The incident they hoped to recreate occurred at Kent State University in Kent, Ohio, in 1970. There, the Ohio National Guard killed four unarmed students and wounded several more during an on-campus protest. Reportedly, the members of the Bleckley County protesting group were prepared to give their lives to save this seventy-nine-acre farm.

The sheriff said, "I knew Oscar. I didn't really know his family. I knew him, and from everything that was being said, in a very short time, I realized I had as much obligation to protect Oscar as I did the bank. The bank was completely legitimate. But saying to protect Oscar, I realized that the people that got involved in the case were using Oscar. It was a terrorist group. The folks were crazy!"

The group appeared on the Lorick farm in early November. Four men from the Heritage Library in Oklahoma, people described as "mercenaries" from Florida and farmers from Georgia and South Carolina camped out in Oscar Lorick's yard. Most of the participants were armed with pistols, semiautomatic rifles and shotguns. They hung an American flag over the carport of the Lorick house, along with a big blue sheet over the front of the house that read, in white letters, "Oscar Stays. Banks Go!!" Someone spray painted "Live Free or Die" and a sign denouncing the Federal Reserve on one of the grain bins across the lane from the Lorick house. Across Highway 26, "Oscar Stays!! Banks Go! Down with the Federal Reserve System" was painted on the roof of a collapsing barn. A boundary was constructed in the Loricks' front yard from rope, hay and ribbon by one of the protestors, and it was referred to as the "dead-fall line."

The sheriff remembered:

> I can't tell you how many foreclosure notices they had gotten. There was no surprise at all. Then after it got started, the group of people trying to tell Oscar, "We're gonna protect you. We're gonna help you keep your farm." They were just playing him. I tried to tell him while I was at the house, "If these people were legit, they'd tell you how they were coming up with the money. They wouldn't be telling you they're gonna keep me from coming on your property to levy on it. If somebody tells you they're gonna put this off for a week or two or give you the money, you can believe them because they're gonna take you somewhere to get the money or to sign the papers." I may think I can do something and find out I can't, but I'm gonna come back and say, "Oscar, I thought I could do this. I thought I could do this. You're gonna have to find another route." They're gonna have to produce. They're gonna have to tell you the route they're going. If they tell you they're talking to First National Bank or CNS Bank, you can talk to that bank and you can talk to whoever they're dealing with. It would help, because they're gonna have to meet you face to face. You're gonna have to fill out some paperwork, or some lawyer's gonna come to your house for you to sign it.
>
> But I told Oscar, "If you have somebody on your lawn with guns, you know something ain't right." I tried to tell him as gently as I could, because he was getting up in age and I can't remember what kind of medical problems he had. But when I would talk to him, I could tell he wasn't up for a conversation.

A man named Bob Ensley lived in Macon and was a crisis specialist with the Justice Department. He had worked on some of the most difficult cases in the civil rights era and later became the go-to expert on church fires throughout the country. Sheriff Coley said:

> He had been contacted, and he called and asked if he could come talk to me. I said, "Sure I'll talk to anybody." He did and wanted to know if he

THE GEORGIA FARMERS' STRIKE

could help me. He gave me his background, who he'd worked for. I told him, "I don't know what to tell you to do if I don't know what I'm gonna do. And I don't even know what I'm gonna need." I told him, "You may be a good communication link to Oscar. The way they're making him believe, there's a good chance they're making Oscar where he doesn't even trust me. Maybe you can keep his trust where we can communicate." And this was way before it was really getting dirty. Because at that point and time, I was maybe thinking about a riot or some kind of damage to the community.

What I was talking about, it was getting dirty; the word I got was they had put bombs, dynamite, whatever in different places on the farm, so if we did start to walk in the house, they could blow us up! I had been briefed, I don't know how many times, how armed these people were. I'd even been told that the group that came in to protect Oscar, if they killed a sheriff, they got one point. And if they killed a federal officer, they got a half a point. And as you're sitting there listening, you're thinking, "This ain't coming to Cochran, Bleckley County." I stayed focused—or tried to.

I called Judge O'Connor. He was our superior court judge. He's the one that signed the order. I went to him and said, "Judge, I don't want to get in no trouble with the court. I want to defuse this situation." And I told him everything I'd been told about the group from Oklahoma. He told me that we would have no trouble. He said, "I know what you're telling me. I understand what you're telling me, and you do what you feel like. If you feel like you need to talk to me; you call me, or you come talk to me." He lived down around Jaybird Springs. When I got through talking to the judge, I felt more comfortable because when you've got a legal process, in just a few days, it's got to be done within the law.

I told my department that the group wanted to meet, and I told them I would go. Everybody around me was telling me, "Don't go." Because the word we had was of being shot; we were told they had high-powered rifles, shotguns and stuff. That's why everybody around me was telling me, "Don't go." I told them, "I'm going." And they tried to arm me, I said, "I'm not taking a gun with me. We're gonna defuse this thing. If I get shot, maybe I'll survive. That's all I know to tell you, but I'm going." They kept telling me, but I said, "There's no question about me going. Because I know how to go, and nothing will happen. I can't tell you there won't be somebody out there with a 30-06 and shoot me or something."

I thought if I stayed on the road, his driveway was concrete, the best I remember. I knew with them driving back and forth on that driveway, there was not a bomb in that roadway or in that driveway. That's what I'm *gonna stay on and where I'm going. When I got inside, we just talked about the situation. I tried to make Oscar feel comfortable, to make him feel like I was his friend. I tried to tell him, "You've got to be careful who you listen to." And I tried to tell him as respectful as I could, "Oscar, these people are using you."*

When asked who from the group was inside the Lorick home when he entered, the sheriff said, "I'm sure some of them were there. I'm positive. I can't tell you who was there. I can tell you I didn't take anybody that was outside my staff with me. We didn't take a weapon with us, period. We didn't even have one in the car. Of course, I never carried a gun, and I never had one in the car with me at no time, before then or after. And I was driving an unmarked car. Oscar, everybody in the county knew my car. I led every funeral with that car. Everybody knows you in a place like Cochran, Bleckley or Pulaski County."

Though the group wanted to have a Kent State–style "incident," it appeared they had picked the wrong county. They faced an unarmed sheriff and an unarmed deputy without so much as a pocketknife or a sharp no. 2 pencil inside their unmarked police car.

19

BLECKLEY COUNTY REBELLION

The situation in Bleckley County was difficult for everyone, especially the Lorick family. One of Oscar Lorick's sons also lived at the barricaded farm and was afraid to go home. He asked to stay with another farmer's family nearby until the standoff was over.

When asked if anyone from the armed group made any comments, pointed a gun or threatened him while he was inside the Lorick house, Sheriff Coley said:

> *I never recall one of them saying anything to me. The guns weren't in the house. The guns were all outside. You could ride by in a car and see one or ten guns. They had them on their shoulder like a guard at a government complex. When you're trying to get somebody to believe, and I would tell my folks, "If I can at least keep him [Oscar Lorick] on an even keel. If I can in some way make him ask himself a question about that group, just to create some doubt. After a while, he's got to see if what I'm telling him makes sense. I may not know it's true, but I know if it makes sense. I was trying to get him out where they wouldn't incorporate with him."*

When asked if he received any offers of help from the community, he responded:

> *I know I had people come to the courthouse that had guns. I had one guy come to the courthouse and had a buffalo gun or something he used when he went to Africa hunting. He didn't come in the courthouse but sent me word*

to come out when I had time. I walked up to the car, spoke—"How you doing? What you need?"—what have you. And saw the guns in the back seat. He told me there were people in the county that would go with me, all I had to do was tell them, "Come on. We're fixing to go to Oscar Lorick's." I told him, "Boss, I love you, but go home! Put these guns back up." That's the very last thing I needed was another gun in the situation! I didn't know how many guns were out there. The bombs. The dynamite. I think the Macon Telegraph *had pictures of people with rifles and shotguns on his lawn. People would ride by and come to the courthouse and say, "Ed, let me tell you what I just saw out there at Oscar's."*

An interesting story came up when I asked if there were any local people who assisted the protesting group. The sheriff said:

I had people out there with him, and I had one guy on probation. The next day or the second day, here came the probation officer telling me he had got a judge to sign a warrant for the guy. He's on probation and out there with a shotgun or high-powered rifle. I forgot. I told him, "Look, take it back to the judge and stop it, or give it to me and I'll go talk to the judge. I knew he was going because I sent him!" I told him to go and to participate as if he was a participant. I told him to do anything they asked him to do except to plant a bomb or dynamite or shoot somebody. If they ask you why you didn't shoot somebody, tell them you didn't recognize them or somebody else was behind them. I tried to go through every event that could come up so that he would have an answer.

I had a man and a woman out there, and I tried to let them coordinate how they went. But I tried to always have someone out there all the time. See, there's not that many people you can send into a place like that because you have to have somebody that won't talk. I told them, "If you say anything and they tell the commander, they're liable to cut your throat right there in Oscar's yard. This is between me and you. I need help to know what's going on." I wanted to know firsthand. Nothing against radio or newspaper, but my people may be reporting what is and the actual conversation, and I was getting them.

They'd leave and go home, and I'd meet them. I'd get the information, sometimes on the phone. But I had to get the probation officer out of the way. We haven't discussed it in years, but for a while, it was funny. He was doing his job. It was probably my fault. I didn't tell him, not because I didn't trust him. I guess I just wasn't thinking, because I was sending him, and I knew I was protecting the man and the woman.

The time came for both sides to meet on Friday, November 15. A lawyer representing the protesters, Sheriff Ed Coley and two of the protesters met in Cochran at the Bleckley County Courthouse.

> *The lawyer for the group, we met at the courthouse at the main, last meeting. Bob Ensley told me, "Whenever you sit down with this group, the lawyer or whoever, you have got to be at the head of the table." I asked him why, because I just as soon been standing up as much as I would sitting down. He told me, "If you're not at the head of the table, you have no respect at the meeting. Even if you have to make somebody get up and say this is your chair. You tell them." I said, "OK."*

The sheriff sat at the head of the table at the start of the meeting. As the negotiations dragged on, a break was called. When the meeting reconvened, Ed Coley found someone sitting in his chair. Although it got uncomfortable for a moment or two, he said, "I remembered what Bob Ensley told me, and I made them get up out of my spot."

> *But on the night I'm telling you about, when the situation died, the lawyer and I were talking, and I asked him, "What do I have to do? What are you asking me to do to get one result?" He asked me what I needed to have happen. I said, "The folks out at Oscar's place (I'm not sure how I referred to them), I want them gone! I don't care where they go, but I want them out of the county. And if you'll do that, I'll give them more time to come up with the money to save this farm." Just like that, he agreed. I told him, "If you don't live up to your word, Oscar Lorick's fixing to be gone from the farm." Because then I realized I had to have some backbone and had to put the pressure on him. I didn't want him to come back the next morning and say, "Well, I tried this and tried that." I told him, "They're gonna have to leave tonight."*
>
> *The lawyer asked me what to do about not serving the papers. I said, "If ya'll will leave that farm tonight." And we left the courthouse and headed toward Second Street. And everything was repeated on the doorsteps so there wasn't any misunderstanding that not a gun or an individual without a gun is left on Oscar Lorick's place.*

The agreement was made, and the circus left Bleckley County that night. Not one protester stayed behind. To prevent any flareups or incidents, the Bleckley County Sheriff's Department stayed in town while the group made their half-mile retreat across the county line. To be sure the situation was over, the sheriff asked for one more favor:

> *And the probationer that helped me, I went to his house and sent him out there under the pretext that "I'm just coming to see what's going on to be sure they were gone." And those county roads, we rode them to be sure there wasn't a bunch of traffic on them. We wanted to be sure they were gone. I told them if they'd leave that night, not just leave Oscar's property but leave Bleckley County, and they left and went somewhere towards Hawkinsville. I used to know the name of the farm they went to in Pulaski County, because they shot all night. There were people from Hawkinsville calling me to complain. "I don't know what to tell you. Hopefully, they'll run out of ammunition." Not being funny; I was dead serious when I said that. There were a few days there that were scary, made you think what the right word is. Those men were really, really upset with that lawyer. When he agreed to it, they were beat. They were beat, and they knew it. When their spokesman, their lawyer, agreed, and they left; they shot all kinds of ammunition that night.*

When asked if he ever discussed the protest with Oscar Lorick, Sheriff Coley said, "He never did bring it up. I know I did not! Once it's over, if you want to bring it up—but I'm not gonna bring it up to you. First thing you know, I'd be said something, then he'd be said something, and he'd want them folks to come back again."

I told him, "I think the way you handled it was perfect, and they ought to write books about you." His response: "I was just proud they were gone! Nobody got hurt. No property was damaged. That was a real winner."

The standoff was something people from Georgia had never experienced before. There were no textbooks or experts and no trained hostage negotiators available. Ed Coley had only four deputies working with him in total. The FBI, ATF and the GBI weren't staged nearby to help. There were rumors of another, larger group of activists camped near the farm, waiting to respond to the sound of gunfire. But the armed group's situation got turned on its head when the opposing force showed up unarmed. How could there be an accidental shooting from an unarmed officer of the law? Although there were interviews with Ed Coley and materials produced about how he handled his situation, the armed standoffs in the next decade didn't play out so well in places like Ruby Ridge, Idaho, and Waco, Texas.

When Monday morning came, the weekend warriors who populated Oscar Lorick's farm had left the state. The news coverage continued as the tactics to save the farm changed from detonators to donations. An individual from south Florida traveled to Cochran with his young wife, who claimed to be a former resident of the town and neighbor of the Loricks'. The individual came with the intention of buying the farm from the bank and leasing it back to the family for one dollar a year. Oscar Lorick's wife became suspicious of the man when she noticed him ducking into the Loricks' house every time the cameras were running. As soon as the businessman's face appeared on national television, a detective from Florida called the Bleckley County Sheriff's Office. The caller recognized the businessman and knew there had been a warrant for his arrest for several months. It seems this good Samaritan had written some bad checks on an elderly person's account without their consent and hadn't returned some rented electronic equipment. He had also rented the only Cookie Monster costume available for miles around from a local rental store and hadn't returned it in over a year. His was the only arrest made associated with the standoff.

The man from South Florida's chances of buying the farm evaporated as soon as he was booked. But that wasn't the end of Oscar Lorick's story. Another stranger came forward and arranged a news conference with Mister Lorick. This man wore a ski mask and referred to himself as A.N. American. He offered to help fundraise to get the farmer back on his feet. To prove he was serious, the stranger gave Lorick his Rolex watch. The watch was sold and used to pay $7,000 on the debt. As soon as the cameras were turned off, the phones rang, offering help. The stranger's poor disguise was soon abandoned to reveal his identity as Frank Argenbright, a philanthropist and entrepreneur in airport security services from Atlanta.

The fundraising went along smoothly and gained a lot of exposure. The Bronner Brothers Hair Care Company donated a significant amount to the bank note, as did the Kroger Company. The donations were enough to hold off foreclosure until they began to dry up in the very critical last few days before the bank's deadline of April 18. Frank Argenbright made one final desperate plea to the public for the remaining $30,000.

On Saturday, April 12, 1986, state troopers and Bleckley County sheriff Ed Coley were called to a huge gathering at the Lorick house on Highway 26. This time, they came to direct traffic when over five hundred people showed up to help the family burn the farm's mortgage in the yard after paying off the entire debt. Using an additional $9,000 collected to buy seed and fertilizer, Oscar Lorick had big plans for 1986. To help the farm, Frank Argenbright purchased a Ford tractor that had been repossessed from a Burke County farmer and presented it to Oscar at the televised event.

Nathaniel Bronner from the Bronner Brothers Hair Care Company spoke at the event that included a picnic provided by the Kroger Company.

Down the road toward Hawkinsville, the grain bin with "Live Free or Die" and "No Fed Res Sys" painted on the side still stands across the dirt path from the Lorick house. The silver paint is partly shaded by overgrown trees, but it has lasted almost forty years. Whether the writing has been retouched or was just done with good paint remains a mystery. The Lorick family also remains on the land that was under siege for a few tense days in November 1985.

In January 1986, sheriffs in South Georgia were eager to avoid a repeat of the events that occurred in Bleckley County. On January 3, the sheriff of Dooly County discreetly evicted a woman landowner from her farm using a roadblock before a posse could be formed to challenge him. Later that month, a farmer was issued an eviction notice from the Turner County Sheriff after failure to repay a debt of over $350,000 on his 685-acre farm. Even after a foreclosure notice in July 1985, the farmer sent word to the sheriff that he wasn't going to leave his farm. The sheriff, Lamar Whiddon, became concerned about the situation when he was told the farmer had attended an NFPMPU meeting the previous night, so he had a deputy stake out the place on Friday morning. When the deputy reported that the farmer had left the property and Turner County, the entire sheriff's department went to work. A roadblock was set up in front of the house while all the family's possessions were packed into moving vans and stored offsite or left on the side of the road. The GBI and Georgia State Patrol were called in to help with the move. Not long after the move started, many of the same farmers who had camped out on Oscar Lorick's farm appeared at the roadblock wearing their NFPMPU caps, but they could only watch and scowl. When asked about his tactics, the sheriff told the *Macon Telegraph*, "We wanted to do it as quietly as possible. We wanted as little company as possible."

A widow near Dudley got some needed publicity in her case against eviction in early June, but it was too little too late, even with help from Jesse Jackson. The landowner's husband had died twenty years earlier, so she rented out her 377-acre farm to other farmers to earn money. After hitting the same stretch of lean years and bad weather as everyone else, she was foreclosed on by the Federal Land Bank, due to a debt of nearly $200,000. While coming back through town after supporting a candidate for mayor in Savannah, Mr. Jackson stood with the widow, Iverline Payne, as the auction was conducted on the Laurens County Courthouse steps. Along with friends and family, she was supported by the attendance of Oscar Lorick and Tommy Kersey.

Mrs. Payne's son presented her with a briefcase containing $20,000. FLB bid the reserve price of $199,103, which was the amount of debt that was owed. Tommy Kersey bid $199,104 but in "fractional reserve notes." Mrs. Payne's son argued he had the only legal bid, because the land purchase had to be made in cash. The official in charge didn't accept his argument, voided Kersey's bid and awarded the deed back to the FLB. When the sale was over, Mister Jackson accompanied Mrs. Payne back to the foreclosed property and vowed to continue to fight for her farm.

At the end of the 1986 fiscal year, the Federal Land Bank was working through over two hundred foreclosures in Georgia alone, holding an unpaid debt load of nearly $40 million. FmHA had over eighty-five thousand loans in Georgia, with over half of them past due and over twenty thousand in foreclosure. The Production Credit Association had fewer than eighty loans in foreclosure. Georgia farmers were tied with Louisiana for the highest percentage of debts in delinquency at 54 percent.

In May 1987, Tommy Kersey closed the NFPMPU office and closed the books on the farm strike in Georgia. He told reporters that he had spent $500,000 of his own money on the strike over the last ten years and needed to do something else. With a large photograph of tractors in the snow on the National Mall from 1979 and an article about the Bleckley County standoff on the wall, he seemed to reach a low point and pondered if anything he had done really changed anything. He then informed the group that he would change directions and start selling insurance in Unadilla.

20

AN UNIMAGINABLE SACRIFICE

Ever since Eli Whitney moved to Georgia and invented the cotton gin, cotton has been king. After a couple of wars and one hundred years later, the boll weevil invaded Texas from Mexico and didn't stop its migration of destruction until it ran out of bolls to chew. For decades, there wasn't anything to prevent the insect's destruction. Then a doctor's son from Waynesboro invented a compound that gave farmers a fighting chance. The doctor, named Dr. Hill, owned around six thousand acres, planted mostly in cotton, and operated his own steam-powered cotton gin, warehouse and store on the property. In those days, doctors had to make the prescriptions they wrote out for their patients from scratch. Dr. Hill's son, Dozier, used some of the chemicals in his father's apothecary to work up a boll weevil killer he called Hill's Mixture. The product was very successful, especially since everyone from Virginia to Texas had the same problem. Soon, a factory was built in Waynesboro to produce this highly sought insecticide.

In the 1980s, about 1,600 acres of the original farm, in its fourth generation, was still worked by the family, led by L.D. Hill, also known as Lenard Dozier Hill III. He had seen a lot of lean times, but the droughts in the 1970s and the high interest rates that followed almost did him in. The family never considered the option of selling land that had been passed down through their family for so many years. Finally, Mr. Hill had no other option but to borrow against his precious farm to keep going until things turned around. "You can buy land, and you can trade land. But you just can't sell it. It was almost sacrilegious to us. We've always been conservationists, putting terraces in and stuff. When my father borrowed money on the land to farm, he only borrowed like one hundred dollars an acre. So, that was the most he'd ever owed on it. So, farming in the eighties went from bad to worse. The economy had gotten really bad, so he borrowed the money from Federal Land Bank," said Leonard Hill IV, L.D. Hill's son.

Leonard Hill did what many of the Burke County residents did in those days, he worked at the Savannah River Site in South Carolina and planted pine trees in the winter months.

I was planting trees for Stone Container Corporation. It was fairly common to plant about 2,200 acres in the winter. So, I was talking to them, and they had a program where they would lease your land for thirty years and grow timber on it. And they would lease all of it. They would go in, and you would sell all your timber. They'd come in and they'd clear cut it. Then they'd pay the cost to plant and everything. I think they were paying thirty, forty, fifty dollars an acre, which was a good deal. It was per year, and they would sign a contract for thirty years. So, with the contract, the little bit that we owed would have been paid for in eight to ten years. Then my father would have another twenty years of income from it. So, we were really excited about it. We took the deal to the Federal Land Bank, and they would not go along with it. We just could not understand; here was the second-largest paper mill company in the world, just about. So, if they defaulted, you got the trees. It was a win-win for us, but they just would not go along with it.

As the early 1980s nearly ground to a halt, farming conditions didn't improve while the bills grew. In an attempt to pay off the Federal Land Bank loan, L.D. Hill did the unthinkable: he sold a tract of farmland containing four hundred acres. But it didn't bring half the amount he needed to satisfy the lenders. With commodity prices still in tank, he couldn't rely on his farming income to pay off the loan. He was quickly running out of options.

When L.D. Hill's luck finally ran out, the bank foreclosed on his farm and scheduled an auction on the Burke County Courthouse steps at noon on February 4, 1986.

My father had insurance policies, and basically, the day came when the Federal Land Bank foreclosed, and they were gonna auction it off on the courthouse steps. My father had laid all the insurance policies on the bed. I was working third shift at the Savannah River Site, which is in South Carolina and a two-hour ride in the morning and a two-hour ride in the afternoon to get home. And I had just come in when he called me and asked if I was going to the sale, and I said, "No, I am exhausted." Then I said, "I hate I can't do nothing there." I hung the phone up and went back to sleep.

L.D. Hill spread out the insurance policies on the bed and calculated what it would take to save the farm. He totaled up his life insurance policies and hoped the amount would be enough to let the family keep at least one of the three tracts of land. While he was thinking up his plan to save the farm, he didn't discuss it with anyone because of how the life insurance would have to be collected. Unfortunately, life insurance is usually collected by a beneficiary after the policyholder has died. With his wife, Mrs. Annabel, in the kitchen and less than half an hour remaining before the auction started, L.D. Hill sat down on the bed, took a rifle and sacrificed his own life to save his family's farm. He was in his late sixties, in good health and didn't appear to be depressed.

Leonard Hill's mother frantically called him and gave him the news. He quickly collected his emotions, "I called Federal Land Bank, and they were fixing to sell it and told them to stop if they would. I told them what had happened, and they did. It wasn't that he was depressed or anything like that. Like I said, in our family, you just don't sell land. He knew that he didn't have enough to save it all, so he thought he might could save maybe half of it. So, he committed suicide." Within a couple of days, the news of a funeral in Waynesboro covered the state. The minister officiating said he knew there was a reason for it, even if it wasn't immediately clear. He hoped this would expose the problem that led to such a tragedy.

Despite all the circumstances, the Federal Land Bank still planned to liquidate the farm and rescheduled the auction for September. Several of the insurance policies had expired in January without L.D. Hill's knowledge. Though the FLB loan was only about $60,000, there was also a Production Credit Association note that pushed the total above $300,000. And since the whole thing had to be sold in one piece, the family wasn't going to have nearly enough to keep the farm. It looked as though L.D. Hill had died in vain.

So, that's kind of when the news media got a hold of it. Then there was a gentleman named Frank Argenbright. He owns Argenbright Security in

Atlanta, and he handled all the security for the Atlanta Airport up there. So, he called me and said, "Look, I'm gonna try to help you. I don't know what all I can do for you. Come on. Let's talk about it." So, he came down—super nice guy and everything. Several weeks later, he called and said, "Come up to Atlanta. We'll put on a news conference up here." So, we did, and it was me and my mother and, I think, one of my sisters.

At the time, Mr. Argenbright was helping a Black farmer down in Cochran, Georgia, named Oscar Lorick. At the time, Bonner Brothers Hair Care Products was a big donor for Oscar. As a matter of fact, one of the Ford tractors that got repossessed from me, Frank Argenbright bought it and gave it to Oscar. So, they hauled it down there and presented it to Oscar—Bonner Brothers did. Just a real, real nice event down there. So, they said, "We need to go to Atlanta and do another news conference." So, we said, "OK, we'll do it." So, we went back, and at that one, Mr. Argenbright had a secretary named Mrs. Kimsey. Mrs. Kimsey, she was sharp as a needle, she was on it. So, she put it together and everything. She called the TV stations and they did the interview.

ABC broadcast the story nationwide on *Nightline* on August 27. Mrs. Hill was the focal point of the segment, speaking at the press conference from the Argenbright Securities office. Also at the press conference in support of the Hill family was Mr. Oscar Lorick. Leonard Hill remembered:

Donald Trump and his wife were in New York. So, they saw it. This was Ivana, his first wife. Donald Trump saw it and said, "Somebody ought to help that lady." His wife said, "Why don't you get up and do it?" Then he said, "I will." And that was when he called Frank Argenbright in Atlanta, and that's how it got started.

We called the local sheriff and said, "Do you mind checking out this Trump guy? 'Cause we don't know who he is." And you've got to be careful with all folks that call and all the other stuff going on. So, he said, "No, I don't mind." So, he called around, and after about an hour or two later, he called back and said, "This guy's for real, now! Don't botch this up! He's about as straight up as your gonna get." So, we said, "OK, we'll talk to him."

On September 2 and just minutes before the auction started on the Burke County Courthouse steps, Frank Argenbright agreed to buy the farm for $177,000 unless another buyer could be found within the month. The family flew to Trump Tower and met Donald Trump in New York City. During a press conference, Trump gave the family a donation of $20,000 to get things started and promised to help raise the rest. In his book *The Art of the Deal*, Trump tells how he got the September auction postponed by telling the vice-president of the bank that he would bring a lawsuit against him on the grounds that he harassed L.D. Hill until he killed himself. According to Trump, a few minutes later, the man called back and gave him a few more months to work it out.

As the year came to an end, time was running out again. The family had been raising money at a steady pace for a while but was $78,000 short in the middle of December. The farm was still in danger of being auctioned off if the remainder wasn't collected in time. "Then there was another developer in Dallas, Texas, named Tom McCamy, and he donated a good bit towards it. So, Donald Trump went down there, and between the real estate guy and the developer, I think they put a few deals together in Dallas, Texas." Mr. McCamy promised to donate half of the remainder, $39,000, if the public would donate the other half. Before Christmas, the entire amount had been collected. After the remaining portion of debt had been paid, a mortgage burning ceremony was held at Trump Tower on December 23, attended by Annabelle Hill, Donald Trump and Tom McCamy. At the press conference, Mr. McCamy made a statement that echoed back to the beginning of this whole mess. He said the only way out of the current financial situation was for farmers to receive full parity for what they produced. "That's when Trump came down, and they burned the notes at Trump Tower in New York. That's just how it went," said Mr. Hill.

We've continued to farm the place. I've got three daughters. The farm, which I think was originally about 1,600 acres, about 750 acres is what we ended up saving. So, my three daughters helped farm, and then they decided to go to college. I said, "So, you're gonna come back and help me farm?" They said, 'Not no, but h— no! We ain't coming back to farm." They'd done had enough! So, what they didn't know was, since they weren't coming back, they thought, I put all the open acres into CRP longleaf pine trees. They're the ones that had to plant them all. So, I went and bought an old used planter that you sit on and have to bend down and plant the seedling. They ended up planting like 185,000 trees like that. We'd swap around, like they'd plant and I'd drive for a while.

The youngest one went to the University of Georgia then got a grant or a scholarship to go to the Catholic Law School in Washington, D.C. So, she's a lawyer and was in North Carolina doing pro bono work around Chesapeake Bay doing environmental stuff. She's now up in Augusta, Georgia, as the assistant district attorney up there. My oldest daughter is a teacher in the local public school, I think she's closer to twenty years doing that. Then my middle daughter decided to be a hairdresser. The crazy thing is, the hairdresser's making more money than anybody else.

I asked, "Does she use Bonner Brothers Hair Products?"

"No, she doesn't," answered Mr. Hill. I just had to ask.

The farm was saved, and the family has thrived. Though the farm didn't get planted in loblolly pine, it was planted in longleaf pine and stayed in the Hill family against overwhelming odds—with a little help from Donald and Ivana.

BIBLIOGRAPHY

Chapter 1

Allen, Fredrick. "Farmers Demand Parity. Few Understand What It Means." *Atlanta Journal*, December 9, 1977.

Dunning, Lorry. *John Deere Tractor Data Book: Two-Cylinder Models Through 1960*. 1st ed. Osceola, WI: MBI Publishing Co., 1997.

Macon News. "Peanut Crop Faces Cut." March 19, 1977.

Rucker, Walter H. "Parity Is Something Difficult to Explain." *Forsyth County News*, March 29, 1978.

Chapter 2

American Agriculture Movement, Inc. "History of the American Agriculture Movement." http://aaminc.org/history.htm

Atlanta Journal. "Can't Work Miracles, Bergland Tells Farmers." September 23, 1977.

Hilliard, Carl. "Angry Farmers Begin Protest of Farm Policy." *Fort Collins Coloradoan*, September 20, 1977.

McCarthern, Gerald. *From the White House to the Hoosegow*. Canyon, TX: Staked Plains Press, 1978.

Office of the Clerk, U.S. House of Representatives. "Ninety-Fifth Congress." March 24, 2006. https://web.archive.org/web/20060601191832/http://a257.g.akamaitech.net/7/257/2422/26jan20061725/www.gpoaccess.gov/serialset/cdocuments/hd108-222/95th.pdf

Chapter 3

Blum, Deborah. "Protests Prelude to Strike?" *Macon Telegraph*, November 6, 1977.

Jeff Davis County Ledger. "Tractor-Cade Protests Farm Prices, Policy." November 2, 1977.

Macon News. "Farmers on March to Protest Prices." October 29, 1977.

Macon Telegraph. "Tractors Rumble into Statesboro." November 6, 1977. Wire reports.

Montgomery, Bill. "Farmers Snarl Alma Traffic." *Atlanta Journal and Constitution,* October 30, 1977.

Spivey, Marshall. "Nearly 3,000 Tractors Ready for Farmer's Protest Friday." *Statesboro Herald,* November 2, 1977.

Statesboro Herald. "Tractor Routing Planned." November 3, 1977.

Wohlgemuth, Dean. "Bacon Farmer Swaps a Tractor for an Office." *Times-Union,* December 5, 1977.

———. "Small Article Leads Farmer to Movement." *Times-Union,* December 6, 1977.

Chapter 4

Abernathy, Russell. "Farmers 'Ain't Had Much Luck Yet.'" *Macon News,* December 9, 1977.

Atlanta Journal-Constitution. "Bergland to Answer Farmers' Questions in Ashburn, Millen." December 1, 1977.

———. "Farmers Stage Protests." December 4, 1977.

Bush, Luthene. "Destroying Evidence Was a Judgement Decision." *Macon News,* November 23, 1978.

Cox, Calvin. "The Week at a Glance." *Atlanta Journal-Constitution,* November 6, 1977.

Goolrick, Chester. "20,000 Farmers Invade Plains." *Atlanta Journal-Constitution,* November 26, 1977.

Hawkinsville Dispatch. "Rally Draws Few Tractors, Gets String Support." November 16, 1977.

Houston Home Journal. "Farm Protest Coming to Perry." November 10, 1977.

———. "Houston Farmers Join Plains Tractorcade." November 24, 1977.

Macon News. "Striker Says Food Shortages Coming." November 27, 1977.

Macon Telegraph. "Farmers Will Support Strike." November 17, 1977.

Trocheck, Kathy. "Protest Comes to Savannah." *Savannah Morning News,* November 20, 1977.

Verner, Chris. "Farmers' Big Wheels Roll into Hawkinsville." *Macon Telegraph,* November 13, 1977.

Chapter 5

Anderson Independent. "Farmers Gather in Jefferson, Plan Georgia Protest." December 9, 1977.

Atlanta Journal-Constitution. "Farmers Stage Protests." December 4, 1977.

———. "5 States See Protests by Farmers." December 4, 1977.

———. "Governor Proclaims Farm Day." December 9, 1977.

Baksys, Sandy. "Tractor Trek to Dublin Left Out in Cold." *Macon Telegraph-News*, December 9, 1977.

Goolrick, Chester. "Farmers Shiver, Tractors Poised." *Atlanta Journal-Constitution*, December 10, 1977.

———. "Tractors Chug into Unadilla." *Atlanta Journal-Constitution*, December 9, 1977.

Goolrick, Chester, and Stuart Emmrich. "The Tractors Are Coming!" *Atlanta Journal-Constitution*, December 8, 1977.

King, Barry. "20,000 Plan to Ride Tractors to Atlanta." *Atlanta Journal-Constitution*, December 6, 1977.

Macon Telegraph-News. "Watch out Macon; Tractors are Rolling." December 8, 1977.

Rogers, DeWitt. "'Sympathetic' to Farm Protests, Goldkist Says." *Atlanta Journal-Constitution*, December 3, 1977.

Chapter 6

McCash, Selby. "Won't Back Down on Strike Threat, Farm Chiefs Vow." *Macon Telegraph-News*, December 11, 1977.

Montgomery, Bill. "Cold Took Heat Out of Pep Rally." *Atlanta Journal-Constitution*, December 11, 1977.

Robbins, Peter. "Tractors Roll into Macon." *Macon Telegraph-News*, December 9, 1977.

Chapter 7

Easters, Melita. "Hearing Could Affect Farm Pickets." *Tifton Gazette*, December 12, 1977.

Fisher, Robert. "Carter Refuses Public Talk." *Macon News*, December 24, 1977.

Goolrick, Chester. "Farmers Getting Ready for Next Step: Strike." *Atlanta Journal-Constitution*, December 12, 1977.

———. "Strike Second Day." *Atlanta Journal-Constitution*, December 16, 1977.

Goolrick, Chester, and Frank Wells. "Nation's Farmer Strike." *Atlanta Journal-Constitution*, December 15, 1977.

Lewis, Nancy. "Farm Leaders Get Sympathy from Carter." *Atlanta Journal-Constitution*, December 25, 1977.

Robbins, Peter. "Farmer Head for Plains, Hoping to See President." *Macon News*, December 23, 1977.

———. "U.S. Judge Rules Against Farmers." *Macon News*, December 15, 1977.

Schlatter, Lee Ann. "Judge Won't Restraint Picketers." *Macon News*, December 20, 1977.

Statesboro Herald. "Egg Truck Is Target of Sniper." December 23, 1977.

———. "No 'Quick Fix' on Farm." December 16, 1977.

———. "Two Arrests Mar Opening of Strike." December 14, 1977.

Webb, Craig. "Bergland Backs Farmer Strike." *Statesboro Herald*, December 16, 1977.

Wells, Frank. "Pig Farmers Bar Plant Gate." *Atlanta Journal-Constitution*, December 21, 1977.

Chapter 8

Georgia Southern and Florida Railway Co., et al. v. Leighton Kersey, et al. U.S. District Court, CIV-77-209-MAC. Merry Ann Finch, Macon Federal Court, December 15, 1977.

Klinka, Karen. "State, Federal Lawmen Move." *Statesboro Herald*, December 15, 1977.

Chapter 9

Allen, Fredrick. "Larry Flynt Buys Plains Newspaper." *Atlanta Journal-Constitution*, January 6, 1978.

Bonner, Christopher, and Betty Wells. "Farmers See Icy Carter." *Atlanta Journal-Constitution*, February 15, 1978.

Boyd, Bill. "Farmers Gambling in Ouster Effort." *Macon News*, January 7, 1978.

———. "Reynolds Loses Farm Bureau Job After 8 Years." *Macon News*, December 6, 1978.

———. "Reynolds Sure of Outcome in Farm Bureau Election." *Macon News*, December 6, 1978.

Brenner, Bernard. "Farmers Take Over Farm Chief's Office." *Atlanta Journal-Constitution*, January 20, 1978.

Goolrick, Chester. "Eggs, Demands Batter Farm Bureau in Macon." *Atlanta Journal-Constitution*, February 24, 1978.

Hume, Craig R. "Farmers Cited in Clash." *Atlanta Journal-Constitution*, January 19, 1978.

———. "Farmers Take Plea for Parity to Senate Panel." *Atlanta Journal-Constitution*, February 24, 1978.

Macon News. "Farmers Don't Tear Up Towns." January 20, 1978.

———. "Reynolds Faces Challenge." October 3, 1978.

———. "Wilcox Farmers Join in Move to Oust Reynolds." March 15, 1978.

Roberts, Mike. "No Matter How Long It Takes." *Red and Black*, January 17, 1978.

Schlatter, Lee Ann. "Angry Farmers Ask Reynolds to Resign." *Macon News*, January 5, 1978.

Selma Times-Recorder. "Tractorcade from Texas in Ohio on Way to D.C." January 16, 1978.

Chapter 10

American Agriculture News. "McAllen Reviewed." Summer 1978.

Boyd, Bill. "Farmers Released on Bond." *Macon News*, March 4, 1978.

Galveston Daily News. "Farmers Meet Briscoe, Go Home to Plan Efforts." March 5, 1978.

Jakush, Judy. "Area Farmers Witness Friends' Texas Arrests." *Macon News*, March 2, 1978.

Tyler Morning Telegraph. "Striking Georgia Farmers to Block McAllen Bridges." February 25, 1978.

Chapter 11

American Agriculture News. "American Ag National Meet Productive." April 27, 1978.

———. "American Agriculture Adopts 5 Points." Summer 1978 SE.

———. "USDA Locks Farmers Out of Building." March 21, 1978.

———. "Washington Got Farmers Goats." March 21, 1978.

Galveston Daily. "Bergland Defends His Policy in Meeting with Farmers." March 18, 1978.

Hume, Craig R. "Farmer Bill Dies in House." *Atlanta Journal-Constitution*, April 13, 1978.

Macon News. "Striking Farmers Plow Under Crops." March 22, 1978.

Town Talk. "Farmers Stage Sit-In in a USDA Building." March 17, 1978.

Willis, Myra. "Georgia Organizes." *American Agriculture News*, June 1, 1978.

Chapter 12

American Agriculture News. "Four Die for American Agriculture." January 9, 1979.

Bevins, Bill. "Protesting Farmers Converge on Plains." *Macon News*, December 23, 1978.

Davis, Peter. "Troopers, Farmers Scuffle." *Atlanta Journal-Constitution*, December 23, 1978.

Goolrich, Chester. "Farmers Protest Prices at Unadilla Tractor Rally." *Atlanta Journal-Constitution*, November 10, 1978.

Macon News. "Farmers, Taiwanese Show Carter Their Ire." December 24, 1978.

Telfair Enterprise. "Farmer Appreciation Day Held." December 13, 1978.

Times Argus. "Farmers, Troopers Tangle in President's Hometown." December 23, 1978.

Chapter 13

American Agriculture News. "And They're Off!" January 23, 1979.

———. "Tractorcade Chugs Onward Toward Washington DC." January 30, 1979.

———. "Tractorcade Will Push for 90% Parity Resolution." November 28, 1978.

Atlanta Journal-Constitution. "Talmadge to be Lead Witness at Ethics Hearing." April 2, 1979.

Cotterell, William. "Talmadge on Alcohol." *Red and Black*, February 27, 1979.

Greenblatt, Jim. "Farmers Are Rolling for Their Livelihood." *Macon News*, January 25, 1979.

McCathern, Gerald. "Tractorcade Date Changed." *American Agriculture News*, January 9, 1979.

Seabrook, Charles. "Breaker 1-9, Tractorcade. Where's Them Texas Boys At?" *Atlanta Journal-Constitution*, January 28, 1979.

————. "8,000 Angry Farmers Ready for Washington?" *Atlanta Journal-Constitution*, February 4, 1979.

Chapter 14

Eason, Henry. "Bergland Blasts Farmers." *Atlanta Journal-Constitution*, February 2, 1979.

Fremont Tribune. "Farmers Arrested." February 6, 1979.

Chapter 15

American Agriculture News. "AAM Testifies on Mall Damage." March 20, 1979.

————. "Farmers Drive Tractors Through USDA Building." February 20, 1979.

————. "Farmers Make Impact on Washington, D.C." February 12, 1979.

————. "Farmers Rescue Washington After 20" Snow." February 27, 1979.

Andel, Adam. "The Editor: HHJ Reader Tells What Really Happened in DC." *Houston Home Journal*, March 29, 1979.

Atlanta Journal-Constitution. "Bergland, Farm Protest Leaders Meet but Resolve Nothing." February 9, 1979.

————. "Farmers' Protest Cost Estimated At $1 Million." February 10, 1979.

B.B. "Go, Tommy Kersey!" *Houston Home Journal*, July 12, 1979.

Christensen, Jean. "AAM About to Lose Political Virginity." *Salinas Journal*, March 8, 1979.

————. "AAM: Pride in Leaderlots." *Garden City Telegram*, March 6, 1979.

Eason, Henry. "Farmers Could Lose by Winning." *Atlanta Journal-Constitution*, February 9, 1979.

Harvey, Paul. "Paul Harvey Says a Bushel of Wheat for a Barrel of Oil." *American Agriculture News*, May 15, 1979.

————. "Paul Harvey Says Next Battlefield to Be the Farm." *American Agriculture News*, December 25, 1979.

Hillgren, Sonya. "Tractors Banned at White House." *Atlanta Journal-Constitution*, February 25, 1979.

Macon News. "Last Tractors Removed from Capitol." March 7, 1979.

————. "Nuclear Leakage 'Serious.'" March 29, 1979. Wire Report.

Montgomery Advertiser. "Farmers March on Washington Post." February 17, 1979.

Chapter 17

American Agriculture News. "AAM Inc. & Grassroots Agree to Co-exist." January 25, 1983.

———. "Farm Implement Makers Are in Financial Crunch." June 2, 1983.

———. "Farm Sale Draws Crowd." January 11, 1983.

———. "John Deere Loses Heavily." June 14, 1983.

———. "Land Stacks Up in FmHA's Hands." October 18, 1983.

———. "Why We Weren't at the Convention." January 25, 1983.

Atlanta Journal-Constitution. "400 Dealers Will BE Eliminated by IH Sale." November 28, 1984.

———. "Harris Seeks Farm Support." February 13, 1985.

———. "Harvester Net Loss $200 Million." May 21, 1982.

———. "IH Reaches Debt Accord." December 16, 1983.

———. "Protesters Fail to Stop Auction of Two Farms." July 3, 1985.

DeVault, Russ. "Save the Farm. Benefit's Organizers Hope Show Will Reap a Harvest of Wealth." *Atlanta Journal-Constitution*, September 12, 1985.

Goldberg, Steve. "Singing Farmers Block Forced Sale of Man's Land." *Macon Telegraph and News*, February 6, 1985.

Macon News. "Farmer Protest Turns Foreclosure Sale into a Melee." January 5, 1983.

Macon Telegraph and News. "Georgia 3rd in Delinquent FmHA Loans; Ruling Halts Foreclosure." August 17, 1984.

Milner, Elliott. "Scuffle at Courthouse Fails to Stop Farm Foreclosures." *Macon Telegraph and News*, March 6, 1985.

Mooney, Brenda. "Fate of Thousands Hangs on Judgment in Lawsuit." *Atlanta Journal-Constitution*, March 19, 1982.

Telfair Times. "Sale of Foster Farm Blocked in Telfair." February 27, 1985.

Chapter 18

Cochran Journal. "Armed Protesters Leave When Sheriff Delays Eviction." November 20, 1985.

———. "Bleckley Farmer Faces Eviction." November 13, 1985.

———. "Legal Notices." February 27, 1985.

Gibbs, Judy. "Bleckley Farm Protester Is Banker's Son Who Is Using His Wealth to Fight the Banks." *Macon Telegraph and News*. November 24, 1985.

Minor, Elliott. "Scuffle at Courthouse Fails to Stop Farm Foreclosures." *Macon Telegraph and News*, March 6, 1985.

Powers, Pat. "Armed Farmers Vow to Block Eviction." *Macon Telegraph and News*, November 15, 1985.

Chapter 19

Beasley, David. "Activist Kersey Will Close Farm Pricing Union Office, Sell Insurance." *Atlanta Journal-Constitution*, May 10, 1987.

———. "Farm Eviction Surprises Protesters." *Atlanta Journal-Constitution*, January 25, 1986.

————. "Jackson Backs Widow as Farm Is Foreclosed." *Atlanta Journal-Constitution*, June 4, 1986.

Bradford, Cathy. "Falling Under the Gavel." *Macon Telegraph and News*, August 11, 1986.

Cochran Journal. "Atlanta Man to Raise Funds for Lorick." December 4, 1985.

————. "Buyer of Lorick Farm Arrested." November 27, 1985.

————. "Lorick Burns Mortgage." April 16, 1986.

————. "Payment made on Lorick Farm." April 2, 1986.

Post, Audrey. "Their Eviction Came Through 'Back Door.'" *Macon Telegraph and News*, February 6, 1986.

Wren, Dahlia. "Jackson Joins Widow in Fight to Save Farm." *Macon Telegraph and News*, June 4, 1986.

Chapter 20

Harrell, Bob. "Farmer's Suicide Wasn't Enough to Halt Foreclosure on his Land." *Atlanta Journal-Constitution*, August 7, 1986.

Macon Telegraph and News. "God Will Use Farmer's Suicide, Pastor Tells Mourners at Funeral." February 7, 1986.

Painton, Priscilla. "Farmer's Suicide Likely Won't Save His Land." *Atlanta Journal-Constitution*, February 24, 1986.

Schwartz, Jerry. "Farmer's Widow to Celebrate 'Goodness in Men's Hearts.'" *Macon News*, December 24, 1986.

Walston, Charles. "'Texas Oil Baron' Assists Widow in Fight to Save Farm." *Atlanta Journal-Constitution*, December 5, 1986.

————. "Tycoon Rescues Family of Farmer Who Killed Himself." *Atlanta Journal-Constitution*, September 3, 1986.

ABOUT THE AUTHOR

Lee Lancaster works with the Georgia Department of Agriculture as a contributing writer for the *Farmers and Consumers Market Bulletin*. His "Georgie's Drive" is a feature about Georgia agriculture and rural history, appearing biweekly since 2017. He also serves as a marketing specialist for Vidalia onions and coordinates the Baby Barn program at the Georgia National Fair in October.

Lee attended ABAC for only two years before moving on to the University of Georgia during the Donnan era or Carter administration—Quincy, that is. In spite of that, he still roots for the Dawgs. When he was not attending football games, he was studying agriculture and cleaning chicken houses.

His strong interest in agriculture comes from his family, which has been in involved in farming since Adam and Eve shared an apple. Granddaddy W.D. Knowles was thought to be John Deere by local children in Milan for many years, because he sold tractors, combines and plows. The family has raised Polled Hereford cattle since the mid-1980s.

Lee lives in Eastman with his wife, Keri, two children, Nate and Caroline, and two dogs, Morty and Noodle. The family can be found at Siloam Baptist Church every Sunday and Wednesday.

Visit us at
www.historypress.com